Schöningh



Discover ...

TOPICS FOR ADVANCED LEARNERS

edited by Engelbert Thaler

# The American Dream
## Inventing a Nation

by Hannspeter Bauer

Sprachliche Betreuung: Alexandra Rieb/www.arlanguages.com



www.schoeningh-schulbuch.de
Schöningh Verlag, Jühenplatz 1–3, 33098 Paderborn



Druck 5 4 3 2 1 / Jahr 2013 12 11 10 09
Die letzte Zahl bezeichnet das Jahr dieses Druckes.

Umschlaggestaltung: Franz-Josef Domke, Hannover
Umschlagfoto: © vario images/Tetra Images
Druck und Bindung: westermann druck GmbH, Braunschweig

ISBN 978-3-14-040086-2

# Contents

# Getting started

The United States has been a land of many dreams. What is behind these dreams? Do they still come true, or have they ever come true at all?
Have a look at these pictures. What ideas or associations come to your mind? Complete the mind map.

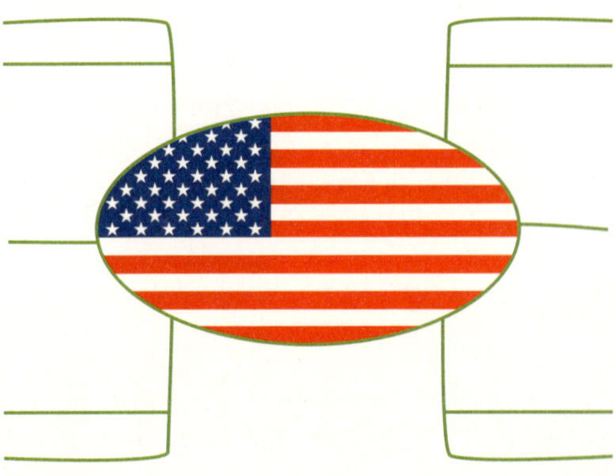

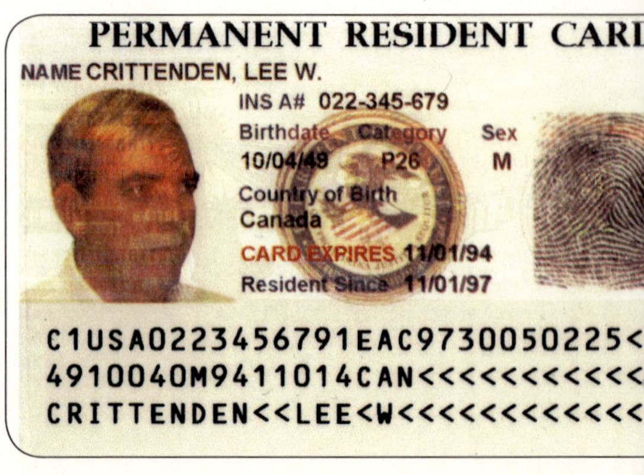

Thought for Food

# Foundations of a Dream

## The Declaration of Independence

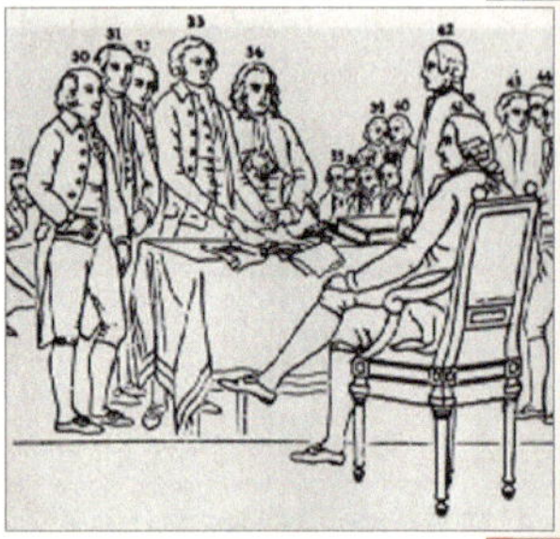

The group standing in the middle presenting the document, consists of (from the left):
John Adams
Roger Sherman
Robert R. Livingston
Thomas Jefferson
Benjamin Franklin. Also standing:
Charles Thomson (Secretary) and sitting:
John Hancock (President of the Continental Congress)

John Trumbull, *Declaration of Independence*, 1817–1819

**Describing a historical painting:**

1. Give a description of the painting (room, decorations, persons, etc).
2. Which group is the most prominent in the picture?
3. How has this been emphasised by the painter?

Before you read

Use the Internet to find out more about the five persons standing in the middle of the painting.

- Give a brief abstract of their lives.
- Why are they so prominent in this scene (historical background)?
- One of them hasn't signed the "*Declaration of Independence*." Who is it and why?
- John Hancock's signature is the first and most flamboyant under the *Declaration*. What was his role at this time? Sketch a short history of the man.

**IN CONGRESS, July 4, 1776.**

**The unanimous[1] Declaration of the thirteen united States of America,**

When in the Course of human events[2] it becomes necessary for one people to dissolve[3] the political bands which have connected them with another and to assume[4] among the powers of the earth, the separate and equal station[5] to which the Laws of Nature and of Nature's God entitle[6] them, a decent respect to the opinions of mankind requires that they should declare the causes which impel[7] them to the separation.
We hold these truths to be self-evident[8], that all men are created equal, that they are endowed[9] by their Creator with certain unalienable[10] Rights, that among these are Life, Liberty and the pursuit of Happiness[11]. – That to secure[12] these rights, Governments are instituted among Men, deriving[13] their just[14] powers from the consent[15] of the governed, – That whenever any Form of Government becomes destructive of these ends[16], it is the Right of the People to alter or to abolish it, and to institute new Government, laying its foundation on such principles and organizing its powers in such form, as to them shall seem most likely[17] to effect their Safety and Happiness. [...]

**Thomas Jefferson, 3rd President (1801 – 1809). He drafted the Declaration of Independence (1776).**

---

1 **unanimous** all agreeing 2 **the Course of human events** (here) history 3 **to dissolve** to end 4 **to assume sth.** to take sth. up, to begin to have or use sth. 5 **station** position 6 **to entitle sb. to sth.** to give sb. the right to sth. 7 **to impel sb. to sth.** to drive sb. to sth. 8 **self-evident** obvious 9 **to endow sb. with sth.** to provide sb. with sth. 10 **unalienable** (old use) = inalienable, impossible to give or take away 11 **pursuit of Happiness** *Streben nach Glück, Zufriedenheit, existentieller Sicherheit* 12 **to secure sth.** to guarantee sth. 13 **to derive sth. from** *etwas herleiten von* 14 **just** (adj. → noun: justice) *gerecht* 15 **consent** permission, agreement 16 **whenever ... these ends** *wenn je eine Regierungsform sich als diesen Zielen abträglich erweist* 17 **in such form, as to them shall seem most likely** in whatever way they think they will have the best chance

## Activities

The main ideas of the "Declaration"

1. Write down the message of the *Declaration* in your own words.
2. In groups of four or five agree on one final draft.
3. Thomas Jefferson wrote the first draft of the *Declaration* combining philosophical ideas of Hobbes, Locke and the later philosophers of the Enlightenment, like Rousseau. Research (→ e.g. *Wikipedia*) these philosophers and their theories and draw a poster of the main ideas/concepts.

The "Pursuit of Happiness"

4. In the second chapter of his *Second Treatise of Civil Government* (1690) John Locke states: "[...] no one ought to harm another in his life, health, liberty, or possessions."
Jefferson reduced this to the three aspects of "life, liberty and the pursuit of happiness." Whereas "life" and "liberty" are clear concepts, "the pursuit of happiness" is a very broad and unspecified idea. Draw a mind map of what it consists of in your opinion.

# The Bill of Rights (1791)

While working on the Constitution of the United States, Federalists and Anti-Federalists argued about the weakness of the Constitution in protecting civil rights. The Federalists' view that the Constitution guaranteed sufficient freedom was attacked by the Anti-Federalists in numerous articles and publications. Especially the founding fathers John Adams, Thomas Jefferson and John Hancock urged that a "Bill of Rights" amending the Constitution should be passed during the process of ratification. The *Virginia Declaration of Rights*, dating back to June 1776, served as the basic concept.

(Note: the printed text follows the original spelling of the document.)

**Amendment I**

Congress shall make no law respecting[1] an establishment of religion, or prohibiting the free exercise thereof; or abridging the freedom of speech, or of the press; or the right of the people peaceably to assemble, and to petition the Government for a redress of grievances[2].

**Amendment II**

Consider why this ▶ amendment was vital in 1791.

A well regulated Militia[3], being necessary to the security of a free State, the right of the people to keep and bear Arms, shall not be infringed[4].

**Amendment III**

No Soldier shall, in time of peace be quartered in any house, without the consent of the Owner, nor in time of war, but[5] in a manner to be prescribed by law.

Bill of Rights

Congrefs of the United States,
begun and held at the City of New York, on
Wednesday, the fourth of March, one thousand seven hundred and eighty nine.

The Conventions of a number of the States having, at the time of their adopting the Constitution, expressed a desire, in order to prevent misconstruction or abuse of its powers, that further declaratory and restrictive clauses should be added: And as extending the ground of public confidence in the Government, will best insure the beneficent ends of its institution:

Resolved, by the SENATE and HOUSE of REPRESENTATIVES of the UNITED STATES of AMERICA in Congress assembled, two thirds of both Houses concurring, That the following Articles be proposed to the Legislatures of the several States, as Amendments to the Constitution of the United States; all, or any of which articles, when ratified by three fourths of the said Legislatures, to be valid to all intents and purposes, as part of the said Constitution, viz.

Articles in addition to, and Amendment of the Constitution of the United States of America, proposed by Congress, and ratified by the Legislatures of the several States, pursuant to the fifth Article of the Original Constitution.

Article the first ...... After the first enumeration required by the first Article of the Constitution, there shall be one Representative for every thirty thousand, until the number shall amount to one hundred, after which, the proportion shall be so regulated by Congress, that there shall be not less than one hundred Representatives, nor less than one Representative for every forty thousand persons, until the number of Representatives shall amount to two hundred, after which, the proportion shall be so regulated by Congress, that there shall not be less than two hundred Representatives, nor more than one Representative for every fifty thousand persons. [Not Ratified]

Article the second .... No law, varying the compensation for the services of the Senators and Representatives, shall take effect, until an election of Representatives shall have intervened. [Not Ratified]

Article the third ....... Congress shall make no law respecting an establishment of religion, or prohibiting the free exercise thereof; or abridging the freedom of speech, or of the press; or the right of the people peaceably to assemble, and to petition the Government for a redress of grievances.

Article the fourth ..... A well regulated Militia, being necessary to the security of a free State, the right of the people to keep and bear Arms, shall not be infringed.

Article the fifth ....... No Soldier shall, in time of peace, be quartered in any house, without the consent of the owner, nor in time of war, but in a manner to be prescribed by law.

**Amendment IV**

The right of the people to be secure in their persons, houses, papers, and effects[6], against unreasonable searches and seizures[7], shall not be violated, and no Warrants[8] shall issue, but upon probable cause, supported by Oath or affirmation, and particularly describing the place to be searched, and the persons or things to be seized.

**Amendment V**

No person shall be held to answer for[9] a capital, or otherwise infamous[10] crime, unless on a presentment[11] or indictment[12] of a Grand Jury[13], except in cases arising in the land or naval forces, or in the Militia, when in

---

[1] **respecting** concerning [2] **redress of grievances** *Beseitigen/Verminderung von Missständen* [3] **militia** *Miliz, Bürgerwehr* [4] **to infringe** to do something that is against a law or someone's legal rights [5] **but** except [6] **effects** personal belongings, property [7] **seizure** when the police or government officers take away goods [8] **warrant** *Haft- bzw. Durchsuchungsbefehl* [9] **to hold sb. to answer for sth.** to accuse sb. of sth. [10] **infamous** bad or evil [11] **presentment** an accusation of crime [12] **indictment** the act of officially charging someone with a criminal offence [13] **Grand Jury** a group of (usually 12) people in the US who decide whether someone charged with a crime should be judged in a court of law

actual service in time of War or public danger; nor shall any person be subject for the same offence to be twice put in jeopardy of life or limb[14]; nor shall be compelled in any criminal case to be a witness against himself, nor be deprived[15] of life, liberty, or property, without due process of law[16]; nor shall private property be taken for public use, without just compensation.

◀ **The consequences of this very special clause have furnished the plot for numerous films.**

**Amendment VI**

In all criminal prosecutions[17], the accused shall enjoy the right to a speedy and public trial, by an impartial jury of the State and district wherein the crime shall have been committed, which district shall have been previously ascertained[18] by law, and to be informed of the nature and cause of the accusation; to be confronted with the witnesses against him; to have compulsory process for obtaining witnesses in his favor, and to have the Assistance of Counsel for his defence.

**Amendment VII**

In Suits at common law, where the value in controversy shall exceed twenty dollars, the right of trial by jury shall be preserved, and no fact tried by a jury, shall be otherwise re-examined in any Court of the United States, than according to the rules of the common law.

**Amendment VIII**

Excessive bail[19] shall not be required, nor excessive fines imposed, nor cruel and unusual punishments inflicted[20].

◀ **Are electrocution or the gas chamber "cruel" or "unusual punishments"?**

**Amendment IX**

The enumeration in the Constitution, of certain rights, shall not be construed[21] to deny or disparage[22] others retained by the people.

**Amendment X**

The powers not delegated to the United States by the Constitution, nor prohibited by it to the States, are reserved to the States respectively, or to the people.

---

[14] **to put in jeopardy of life and limb** *Leib und Leben in Gefahr bringen* [15] **to deprive sb. of sth.** to take away sth. from sb. [16] **due process of law** following proper legal rules and procedures [17] **prosecution** when a charge is made against sb. for a crime, or when sb. is judged for a crime in a court of law [18] **to ascertain** to determine [19] **bail** money left with a court of law to make sure that a prisoner will return when the trial begins [20] **to inflict** to make sb. suffer sth. [21] **to construe** to understand sth. in a certain way; to interpret [22] **to disparage** *schmälern*

## Activities

A closer look at Civil Rights

1. The 10 Amendments can be divided up into three groups of amendments, corresponding to the specific rights they aim to protect. Make a list and try to find appropriate headings for each of the amendments.
2. The German *Grundgesetz* also protects individual rights. Correlate the rights stated in the First Amendment with the corresponding articles of the German *Grundgesetz*.

3. In groups collect and write down passages from the Amendments that reflect the basic ideas of the *Declaration of Independence* (e.g. "all men are created equal" and the "unalienable rights, [...] life, liberty and the pursuit of happiness").

4. Some passages are closely related to the historical situation at that time. Find these and explain the historical background.

How to amend the 2nd Amendment?

5. The Second Amendment is the most controversial today. The NRA (National Rifle Association) maintains that the right of every American to keep firearms should not be limited, whereas many Americans would prefer more limitations and controls.
   - In groups discuss the Second Amendment and design a pro or contra poster.
   - Stage a debate about the topic.

6. After September 11, 2001 the Bush administration restricted numerous liberties with the aim of higher security. Have a look at the two cartoons.

**warrantless NSA spying** the National Security Agency spying without a legal document signed by a judge
**FISA Court** the Foreign Intelligence Surveillance Act created courts that control electronic surveillance

- In groups choose the one cartoon you think expresses the objection to the restrictions best. Give reasons.
- Write a letter to the editor commenting on the cartoon in view of the *Bill of Rights*.

# America (The Beautiful) (1832)

Samuel Francis Smith

This poem was written by the American author Samuel Francis Smith to the tune of the British National Anthem *God save the King*. He had been asked by a friend to translate a German patriotic song and instead of translating the text he wrote new verse to go with the tune. The song was first performed by a children's choir in Boston on Independence Day 1831. The song/poem belongs to the traditional American heritage and was quoted by Martin Luther King in the last part of his famous speech *I have a Dream*. The song combines the features of a hymn sung in church and the style of early 19th century patriotic poetry.

My country, – 'tis[1] of thee[2],
Sweet land of liberty,
Of thee I sing;
Land where my fathers died;
Land of the Pilgrims' pride,
From every mountain side
Let freedom ring.

My native country, – thee,
Land of the noble free,
Thy[3] name I love;
I love thy rocks and rills[4],
Thy woods and templed hills,
My heart with rapture[5] thrills[6]
Like that above.

Let music swell the breeze,
And ring from all the trees,
Sweet freedom's song;
Let mortal tongues awake,
Let all that breathe partake[7]
Let rocks their silence break,
The sound prolong.

Our fathers' God, – to Thee,
Author of liberty,
To Thee we sing;
Long may our land be bright
With freedom's holy light,
Protect us by Thy might,
Great God, our King.

[1] **'tis** it is [2] **thee** you [3] **thy** your [4] **rill** small stream [5] **rapture** state of being carried away by positive emotion, intense joy [6] **thrill** sharp feeling of excitement [7] **to partake** to share, to take a part

## Activities

Analysing the language of the poem

1. Find and name stylistic devices (see list p. 71 f.). What is their function in the text?
2. Using different colours mark all personal pronouns in the poem. Name the differences between stanzas 1, 2, 3 and 4.

Structuring the poem

3. The poem can be divided into three parts. One stanza clearly stands out as different from the rest of the text. Find a heading for this stanza. In some printed versions of the song this stanza is even left out. How do you judge the importance of this stanza?

The message of the poem

4. Using your findings from task 1 to 3 compare the first and the last stanza. Describe the main differences and changes in topic. Also consider the title of the poem.
5. Throughout the 19th century the song was used as a national anthem (though not officially named as such). Comment whether you think it appropriately conveys the ideas of the American ideals.

# The Star-Spangled Banner

Francis Scott Key

Before you read

Find out more about the origin, history and usage of some other national anthems, like the German *Einigkeit und Recht und Freiheit* or the French *Marseillaise*.

Fort McHenry

This poem was written in September 1814, when the British Army and Fleet attacked the American Army at Fort McHenry during the 2nd War of Independence.

O say, can you see, by the dawn's early light.
What so proudly we hailed at the twilight's last gleaming?
Whose broad stripes and bright stars, thro'[1] the perilous fight,
Over the ramparts[2] we watched, were so gallantly streaming[3]?
And the rockets' red glare, the bombs bursting in air,
Gave proof thro' the night that our flag was still there.
O say, does that star-spangled[4] banner yet wave
Over the land of the free and the home of the brave?

---

[1] **thro'** through [2] **rampart** wall built to defend a fort etc. [3] **streaming** movements of a flag *(wehen)* [4] **spangled** covered with ...

Jasper Johns: *Flag* (1954)

On the shore dimly seen thro' the mists of the deep,
Where the foe's[5] haughty[6] host[7] in dread[8] silence reposes,
What is that which the breeze, over the towering steep[9].
As it fitfully[10] blows, half conceals, half discloses?
Now it catches the gleam of the morning's first beam,
In full glory reflected, now shines on the stream:
'Tis the star-spangled banner: O, long may it wave
Over the land of the free and the home of the brave!

And where is that band[11] who so vauntingly[12] swore
That the havoc[13] of war and the battle's confusion,
A home and a country should leave us no more?
Their blood has washed out their foul footsteps' pollution.
No refuge could save the hireling[14] and slave
From the terror of flight or the gloom of the grave:
And the star-spangled banner in triumph doth wave
Over the land of the free and the home of the brave.

O thus be it ever when free men shall stand
Between their loved home and the war's desolation;
Blest with victory and peace, may the heaven-rescued land
Praise the Power that hath made and preserved us a nation!
Then conquer we must, when our cause it is just.
And this be our motto "In God is our trust!"
And the star-spangled banner in triumph shall wave
Over the land of the free and the home of the brave!

---

[5] **foe** enemy [6] **haughty** arrogant [7] **host** army [8] **dread** great fear [9] **towering steep** high cliff [10] **fitfully** *stoßweise [flattern]* [11] **band** group of persons *(Bande)* [12] **vauntingly** boastfully *(prahlerisch)* [13] **havoc** destruction [14] **hireling** a hired soldier *(Söldner)*

## Activities

A linguistic approach

1. Find the three dominant semantic fields and mark them in different colours. You will find at least two of them in most patriotic songs or speeches. What is their function?

2. Text grammars distinguish two different types of *we*: the "receiver including *we*" and the "receiver excluding *we*". Which one is used in this text, and what is the intended effect?

A look at the message

3. *The Star Spangled Banner* was only adopted by Congress as the national anthem in 1931. At that time it had become quite common to sing it at the opening of official celebrations and sports events.

   Compare *America* and *The Stare Spangled banner*. Make a list of what they have in common and where they differ. Which one do you think is the better national anthem?

4. Line 29 reads: "Then conquer we must, when our cause is just." Discuss whether this is an adequate motto for American foreign policy.

# The Gettysburg Address (1863)

Abraham Lincoln

Delivered on November 19, 1863, by President Abraham Lincoln, this speech commemorated the battle fought at Gettysburg, Pennsylvania, on July 1–3, 1863 between the Union and the Confederate forces during the American Civil War. This is one of the shortest though most famous speeches ever given in American history.

Fourscore and seven years[1] ago our fathers brought forth[2] on this continent a new nation, conceived[3] in liberty, and dedicated[4] to the proposition[5] that all men are created equal.

Now we are engaged in a great civil war, testing whether that nation, or any nation so conceived and so dedicated, can long endure[6]. We are met on a great battlefield of that war. We have come to dedicate a portion of that field as a final resting place for those who here gave their lives that the nation might live. It is altogether fitting and proper that we should do this.

**Note all the negatives ▼ in this passage. What might be the message?**

But, in a larger sense we cannot dedicate – we cannot consecrate[7] – we cannot hallow[8] – this ground. The brave men, living and dead, who struggled here, have consecrated it far above our poor power to add or detract. The world will little note nor long remember what we say here, but it can never forget what they did here. It is for us, the living, rather, to be dedicated here to the unfinished work which they who fought here have thus far so nobly advanced. It is rather for us to be here dedicated to the great task remaining before us – that from these honored dead we take increased devotion to that cause for which they gave the last full measure of devotion; that we here highly resolve[9] that these dead shall not have died in vain; that this nation, under God, shall have a new birth of freedom; and that government of the people, by the people, for the people, shall not perish[10] from earth.

**Fletcher C. Ransom: Lincoln at Gettysburg**

[1] **fourscore and seven years** i.e. (4 x 20)+7 = (that means: in the year 1776) [2] **to bring sth. forth** to produce [3] **to conceive sth.** to form in the mind (a plan etc.) [4] **to dedicate** to devote to sth. (*widmen*) [5] **proposition** statement that expresses a judgement/opinion [6] **to endure** to suffer patiently [7] **to consecrate sth.** to reserve sth. as sacred [8] **to hallow sth./sb.** to honour sb./sth. as holy [9] **to resolve sth.** to decide firmly, to determine [10] **to perish** to be destroyed, to die

## Activities

Analysing a political speech

1. The speech is clearly subdivided into three parts that refer to three different periods of time. Begin a table for your analysis by giving the three parts an appropriate time label.
2. Lincoln expresses several recurrent ideas, underlining them by the repetition of specific words; one of these is the concept of a "nation", another one is "liberty"/"freedom". Find other significant repetitions of words.
3. Use the list of stylistic devices (p. 71 f.) and analyse which rhetorical devices Lincoln uses. Discuss the intended effect upon the listeners.

Reporting from memory

4. You are a reporter working for *The Yankee Gazette* (a "northern" paper of that time). Write a report about the commemorations at Gettysburg. Your readers will be most interested to learn what the President said. Remember that you did not have a tape recorder nor was there any printed text of the speech. So you have to report from memory.

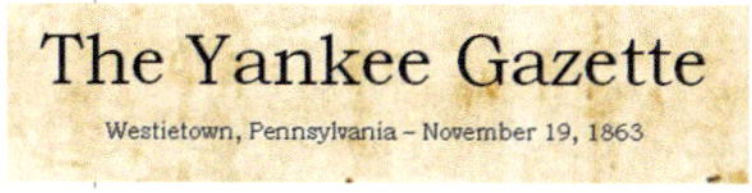


# Taking What's Best from the French

Bill Maher

American history is ever present in public speeches and discussions. The American stand-up comedian and journalist, Bill Maher, looks back at the intentions of the "Founding Fathers" to analyse the USA of today. One of the main features of his comment published in *Newsweek* is undoubtedly irony. So be careful reading the text and distinguish between what he says and what he means!

◀ **Can you think of any historical reasons why he has chosen France as a contrast?**

New rule: Conservatives have to stop rolling their eyes every time they hear the word 'France'. Like just calling something French is the ultimate argument winner. Aw, you want a health-care system that covers everybody and costs half as much? You mean like they have in France? What's there to say about a country that was too stupid to get on board with our wonderfully conceived and brilliantly executed war in Iraq?
Earlier this year, the "Boston Globe" got hold of an internal campaign document from GOP[1] contender[2] Mitt Romney, and a recurring strategy was to tie Democrats to the hated French. It said, in the Machiavellian code of the election huckster[3], "Hillary[4] equals France," and it envisioned bumper stickers that read "FIRST, NOT FRANCE."
Except for one thing: We're not first. America isn't ranked anywhere near first in anything except military might and snotty[5] billionaires. The country

---

[1] **GOP** "grand old party", the Republican Party [2] **a contender** a person who applies for a job, an office; here: a person trying to become the presidential candidate of the Republicans [3] **a huckster** a person who uses aggressive methods to sell sth. [4] **Hillary** referring to Hillary Clinton, at that time most potential presidential candidate for the Democratic Party [5] **snotty** snobbish

Arrogant, ironic or just ▶ typically American as a remark?

Note his idea of ▼ "stealing".

What is his attitude ▼ towards the government in Washington?

that is ranked No. 1 in health care, for example, is France. The World Health Organization ranks America at 37 in the world – not two, or five – 37, in between Costa Rica and Slovenia, which are both years away from discovering dentistry. Yet an American politician could not survive if he or she uttered the simple, true statement, "France has a better health-care system than us, and we should steal it." Because here, simply dismissing[6] an idea as French passes for an argument.

John Kerry? Can't vote for him – he looks French. Yeah, as opposed to the other guy[7],who just looked stupid. I know, if God had wanted us to learn from the Enlightenment[8], he wouldn't have given us Sean Hannity[9]. And I'm not saying France is better than America. Because I assume you've already figured that out by now. I don't want to be French, I just want to take what's best from the French. Stealing, for your own self-interest.

Republicans should love this idea. Taking what's best from the French: You know who else did that? The Founding Fathers. Hate to sink your toy boat, Fox News, but the Founding Fathers, the ones you say you revere[10], were children of the French Enlightenment, and fans of it, and they turned it into a musical called *the* Constitution of the United States. And they did a helluva[11] job, so good it has been said that it was written by geniuses so it could be run by idiots.

But the current administration is putting that to the test. The Founding Fathers were erudite[12], well-read, European-thinking aristocrats – they would have had nothing in common with, and no use for, an ill-read xenophobic[13] bumpkin[14] like George W. Bush. The American ideas of individuality, religious tolerance and freedom of speech came directly out of the French Enlightenment – but, shhh, don't tell Alabama.

Voltaire[15] wrote "men are born equal" before Jefferson was wise enough to steal it. Countries are like people – they tend to get smarter as they get older. Noted military genius Donald Rumsfeld famously dismissed France as part of Old Europe, but the French are ... what's the word I'm looking for? Oh yeah, "mature." We think they're rude and snobby, but maybe that's because they're talking to us[16]. For example, France just had an election, and people over there approach an election differently. They vote. Eighty-five percent turned out[17]. The only thing 85 percent of Americans ever voted on was Sanjaya[18].

Maybe the high turnout has something to do with the fact that the French candidates are never asked where they stand on evolution, prayer in school, abortion, stem cell research or gay marriage. And if the candidate knows about a character in a book other than Jesus, it's not a drawback. There is no Pierre Six-pack[19] who can be fooled by childish wedge issues[20]. And the elec-

---

[6] **to dismiss** to decide that sth. is not worth thinking about [7] **the other guy** in the 2003 elections that was George W. Bush [8] **Enlightenment** *die Aufklärung* [9] **Sean Hannity** conservative talk show host (Fox and radio programmes) [10] **to revere** to feel great respect for [11] **helluva** (colloq.) hell of a = a very good ... [12] **erudite** having great knowledge [13] **xenophobic** feeling dislike for people from other countries [14] **bumpkin** a person from the countryside who seems stupid [15] **Voltaire** French philosopher (1694–1778) of the Enlightenment [16] **talking to us** (here) *uns widersprechen* [17] **to turn out** to participate [18] **Sanjaya (Malakar)** participant in the TV show American Idol (= DSDS in Germany) [19] **Pierre Six-pack** allusion to "John Six-pack", simple minded star in workout videos [20] **wedge issue** political issue of controversial nature, driving a wedge into the population

torate doesn't vote for the guy they want to have a croissant with. Nor do they care about the candidate's private lives: In the recent race, Ségolène Royal had four kids but never bothered to get married. And she's a socialist.

In America, if a Democrat even thinks you're calling him a liberal he immediately grabs an orange vest and a rifle and heads into the woods to kill something. As for the French conservative candidate[21], he's married but he and his wife live apart and lead separate lives. They aren't asked about it in the media, and the people are OK with it, for the same reason the people are OK with nude beaches: because they're not a nation of 6-year-olds who scream and giggle if they see pee-pee parts. They have weird ideas about privacy. They think it should be private. In France, everyone has a mistress. Even mistresses have mistresses. To not have a lady on the side says to the voters, "I'm no good at multitasking."

▼ **Does his description truly express the idea of European democratic attitudes?**

France has its faults – the country has high unemployment, a nasty immigrant problem and all that ridiculous accordion music. But its health care is the best, it's not dependent on Mideast oil, it has the lowest poverty rate and the lowest income-inequality rate among industrialized nations, and it's the greenest, with the lowest carbon dumping and the lowest electricity bill. France has 20,000 miles of railroads that work. We have the trolley at the mall that takes you from Pottery Barn to the Gap. It has bullet trains[22]. We have bullets. France has public intellectuals. We have Dr. Phil[23]. And France invented sex during the day, the *menage a trois,* lingerie and the tongue. And the French are not fat. Can't we just admit we could learn something from them?

---

[21] reference to Nicolas Sarkozy, who then ran for President in France and was elected soon afterwards [22] **bullet trains** high speed trains (the 'TGV') [23] **Dr. Phil (McGraw)** psychologist, author of numerous books on "real life issues" and host of a TV show on CBS

## Activities

Analysing an argumentative text

1. In groups make a list of what Bill Maher says a) about France and b) about the USA. Compare the two lists. What are the main topics?

2. The text is written as an argumentative text giving arguments pro and contra an issue. On the other hand Maher uses a number of images and rhetorical devices that rather classify the article as a persuasive text. Begin by considering the following, then find more:

| | |
|---|---|
| Simile: | an ill-read xenophobic bumpkin like George W Bush (l. 36 f.) |
| Hyperbole: | In France, everyone has a mistress. (l. 65) |
| … | |

What is the intended effect of these rhetorical devices?

Evaluating a historical concept

3. In a fishbowl discussion (four in favour, four against) discuss the statement: "[…] it has been said that it [the Constitution] was written by geniuses so it [the country] could be run by idiots." (l. 31 f.)

# Frontiers of a Dream

## American Progress (1872)

John Gast

### Activities

History in a painting

1. Have a look at the painting. Describe what you see (from left to right).
2. Look up the word "progress" in a dictionary. Which meaning is illustrated by this picture?
3. Imagine you had this picture on an overhead transparency and didn't know which side was the top. How could you tell by the composition of the picture?

# The Significance of the Frontier in American History

Frederick J. Turner

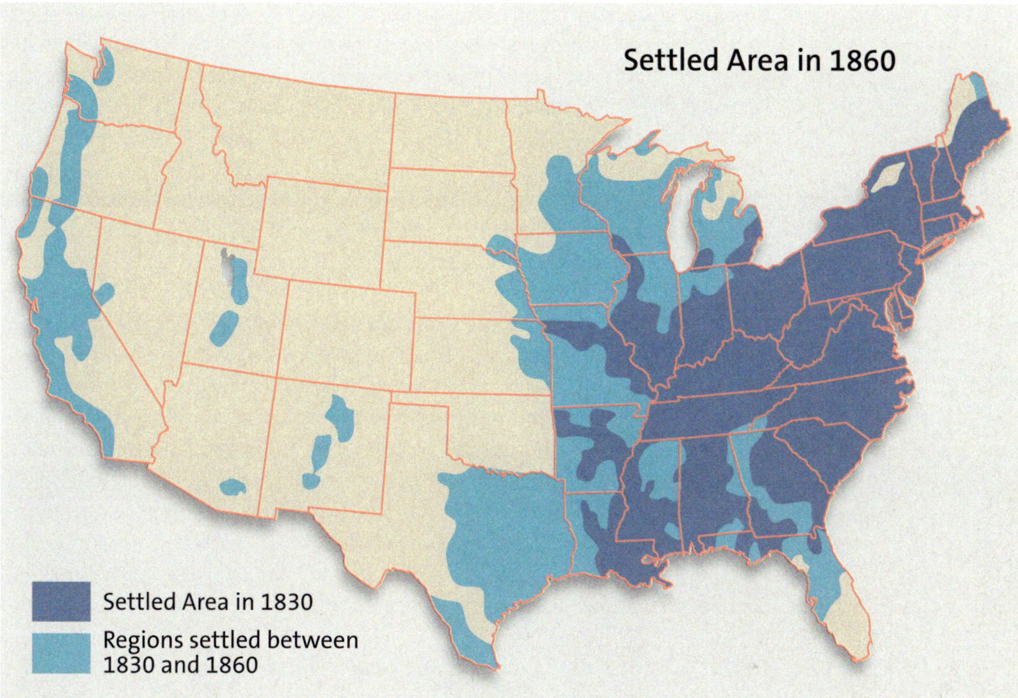


Before you read

Describe the map. What do you notice about the settlement of the continent? Compare your findings with what you said about the painting above.

In a recent bulletin of the Superintendent of the Census[1] for 1890 appear these significant words: "Up to and including 1880, the country had a frontier of settlement but at present the unsettled area has been so broken into by isolated bodies of settlement that there can hardly be said to be a frontier line. In the discussion of its extent, its westward movement, etc., it cannot, therefore, any longer have a place in the census reports." This brief official statement marks the closing of a great historic movement. Up to our own day American history has been in a large degree the history of the colonization of the Great West. The existence of an area of free land, its continuous recession, and the advance of American settlement westward, explain American development.

**▼ Note the different steps of the movement towards the west**

Behind institutions, behind constitutional forms and modifications, lie the vital forces that call these organs into life and shape them to meet changing conditions. The peculiarity of American institutions is the fact that they have been compelled to adapt themselves to the changes of an expanding

[1] **Census** the official count of the country's population

people – to the changes involved in crossing a continent, in winning a wilderness, and in developing at each area of this progress out of the primitive economical and political conditions of the frontier into the complexity of city life. Said Calhoun[2] in 1817, "We are great, and rapidly – I was about to say fearfully – growing!" So saying, he touched the distinguishing feature of American life. All peoples show development; the germ theory of politics[3] has been sufficiently emphasized. In the case of most nations, however, the development has occurred in a limited area; and if the nation has expanded, it has met other growing peoples whom it has conquered. But in the case of the United States we have a different phenomenon. Limiting our attention to the Atlantic Coast, we have the familiar phenomenon of the evolution of institutions in a limited area, such as the rise of representative government; the differentiation of simple colonial governments into complex organs; the progress from primitive industrial society, without division of labor, up to manufacturing civilization. But we have in addition to this a recurrence[4] of the process of evolution in each western area reached in the process of expansion. Thus American development has exhibited not merely advance along a single line, but a return to primitive conditions on a continually advancing frontier line, and a new development for that area. American social development has been continually beginning over again on the frontier. This perennial[5] rebirth, this fluidity of American life, this expansion westward with its new opportunities, its continuous touch with the simplicity of primitive society, has furnished the forces dominating American character. The true point of view in the history of this nation is not the Atlantic Coast; it is the Great West. Even the slavery struggle, [...] occupies its important place in American history because of its relation to westward expansion.

In this advance, the frontier is the outer edge of the wave – the meeting point between savagery and civilization. Much has been written about the frontier from the point of view of border warfare and the chase[6], but as a field for the serious study of the economist and the historian it has been neglected.

**Note the differences ▼ between the American and the European frontier.**

The American frontier is sharply distinguished from the European frontier – a fortified boundary line running through dense populations. The most significant thing about the American frontier is, that it lies at the hither edge of free land. In the census reports it is treated as the margin of that settlement which has a density of two or more to the square mile[7]. The term is an elastic one, and for our purposes does not need sharp definition. We shall consider the whole frontier belt, including the Indian country and outer margin of the "settled area," of the census reports. [...]

The stubborn American environment[8] is there with its imperious summons to accept its conditions; the inherited ways of doing things are also

---

[2] **John Caldwell Calhoun** (March 18, 1782–March 31, 1850) a United States politician (Secretary of War, Vice President of the USA, Senator) from South Carolina [3] **the germ theory of politics** an allusion to the fact that the settlers brought so-far unknown diseases with them, which diminished the native population [4] **recurrence** repetition of the same process [5] **perennial** continuing for a long time; happening again and again [6] **the chase** the run; the drive [7] **a density of two or more to the square mile** > than two people living within a square mile [8] **the stubborn American environment** the difficult climatic or geographical living conditions

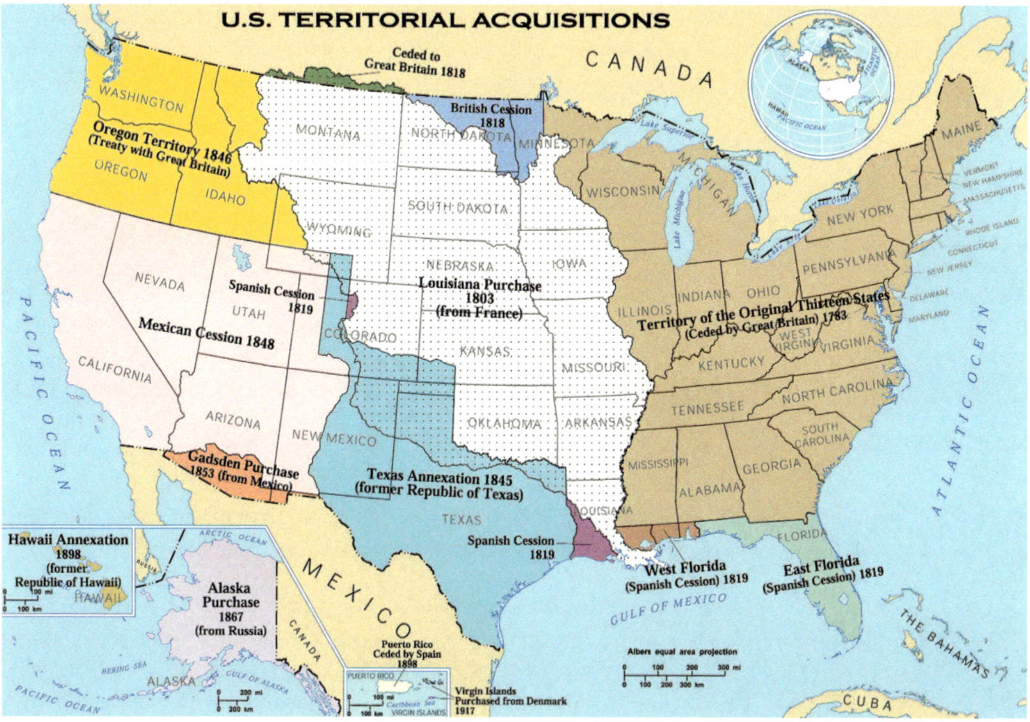


there; and yet, in spite of environment, and in spite of custom, each frontier did indeed furnish a new field of opportunity, a gate of escape from the bondage of the past; and freshness, and confidence, and scorn of older society, impatience of its restraints and its ideas, and indifference to its lessons, have accompanied the frontier. What the Mediterranean Sea was to the Greeks, breaking the bond of custom[9], offering new experiences, calling out new institutions and activities, that, and more, the ever retreating frontier has been to the United States directly, and to the nations of Europe more remotely. And now, four centuries from the discovery of America, at the end of a hundred years of life under the Constitution, the frontier has gone, and with its going has closed the first period of American history.

[9] **the bond of custom** the close relationship through similar ways of behaviour

## Activities

The coining of a term

1. Turner writes: "The peculiarity of American institutions is the fact that they have been compelled to adapt themselves to the changes of an expanding people", (ll. 14 f.). Explain in your own words what he wants to express with this description.

2. The "frontier" had so far only been a mere demographical term. What are the reasons that this text changes it into a "historical concept"?

Evaluating the historical background

3. Turner compares the American colonization to the colonization of the Mediterranean sea by the Greeks. From your historical knowledge explain why he has chosen the Greeks and not the Romans.

4. Turner was right when he stated that "the first period of American history" had been closed. The 1890s mark the turning point for the United States towards a world power. Search information for important historical events concerning the USA in that decade.

## The West

Alexander Keyssar

"The West" is a very general expression to describe the lands west of the Mississippi. The following text is taken from an American history book. The author tries to explain the main motives that drove so many people to seek their happiness in the seemingly endless plains of the newly acquired territories.

The end of the Civil War and the completion of transcontinental railway lines had, in fact, greatly accelerated the development of the trans-Mississippi West. The population of the Pacific and mountain states almost doubled in the 1870s and again in the 1880s; growth in the "west central" states (stretching from Minnesota and North Dakota down to Texas and Louisiana) was even more rapid. By 1910, there were more than 25 million people living west of the Mississippi, 7 million in the Pacific and mountain states alone. At the turn of the century, all of the western territories except Oklahoma, New Mexico, and Arizona had been admitted to the Union as states.

Migrants to the West came from nearly everywhere. Large numbers of Scandinavians, Germans, Irish, and Canadians flocked[1] to the farm states just west of the Mississippi. Mexican immigrants were numerous in the Southwest; California became home to tens of thousands of Chinese immigrants; and thousands of African Americans fled northwest, particularly to Kansas, to escape the repression of the post-Reconstruction[2] South. A majority of the westbound, however, were native-born whites drawn from the middling reaches of American society. Farmers, merchants, and professionals, they traveled in family units, moving from east to west along the same latitude[3]. The railroads made their journeys far briefer and less arduous[4] than they had been before the Civil War, although, like most westerners, they tended to move more than once.

**Why along the same ► latitude?**

---

[1] **to flock** to gather together somewhere in large numbers (usually for birds) [2] **post-Reconstruction** the rebuilding in the Southern States after the Civil War (1860–1864)
[3] **latitude** a line around the globe with same distance to the equator (*der Breitengrad*)
[4] **arduous** involving a lot of difficulty

Why were these people pouring into the West? For most, the answer was straightforward: they wanted land, to settle and to farm. Between 1862 and 1890, nearly 2 million people claimed free land under provisions of the Homestead Act[5]. The typical westward migrant, however, *bought* land from a public land office, a speculator, or the railroads. To subsidize the construction of the railroads, the federal and state governments had given railroad corporations land equivalent in size to the state of Texas, adjacent[6] to the railroad lines themselves. As a result, some of the most desirable land in the West (desirable precisely because of its location) was removed from federal control and had to be purchased from the railroads. In part for this reason – but primarily because most urban workers lacked the capital and the knowledge to get started in farming, whether or not they had to buy land – the Homestead Act never did offer a realistic escape to impoverished, industrial workers.

**◀Could you imagine leaving your home to acquire new land?**

Farming in the region offered new challenges to migrants from the East and Europe. As explorer, scientist, and surveyor John Wesley Powell[7] warned in a report written in 1878, the most important natural fact about the West was its aridity[8]: much of the nation west of the 100th meridian[9] did not receive nearly enough rainfall to sustain conventional methods of farming. As one moved across the prairies of the west central states, annual rainfall totals steadily declined; precipitation in the Great Plains averaged only fifteen to twenty inches a year, less than half the norm in the Mississippi Valley. Farmers on the plains and beyond could not expect to grow wheat, corn, or other crops[10] common in the more humid East.

Yet Powell's warnings were ignored. Encouraged by promoters, farmers flooded into the plains in the 1870s and 1880s. The flat, open grasslands were easy to clear[11] and seemed well suited to new farm implements. Besides, most farmers believed that "rain follows the plow,"[12] that cultivating the land and planting trees would stimulate rainfall. In the 1880s, that belief seemed well founded: the arrival of the farmers coincided with one of the periodic wet cycles on the plains, and crops, including wheat, were plentiful. But when the rains subsided, beginning in 1889, the results were devastating. Crops failed year after year; the earth turned dusty and hard. Some of the region's settlers stayed in place, awaiting the next wet cycle and eventually learning to "dry farm" with

---

[5] **the Homestead Act** (1862) was a federal law that allowed anyone the title to 160 acres of undeveloped land outside of the original 13 colonies, the new law required three steps: file an application, improve the land, and file for deed of title [6] **adjacent** next to [7] **John Wesley Powell** (1834–1902) American geologist, known for his expeditions into the West, the first to pass through the Grand Canyon [8] **aridity** having little or no rain [9] **meridian** line around the world running from the North to the South pole; the 100th meridian runs from North Dakota to Texas, cutting the USA in about the middle of the continent
[10] **crops** plants grown in large quantities, especially for food [11] **to clear** here: *roden*
[12] **rain follows the plow** widely believed theory of the late 19th century that when you work the land the rain will come, too

new methods and new crops. But many left: some counties lost half of their population between 1890 and 1900. One Texas family explained its departure on a sign nailed to their cabin: "Two hundred miles to nearest post office, one hundred miles to wood, twenty miles to water, one mile to hell. God bless our home. Gone to live with the wife's folks."

## Activities

Reasons for the movement West

1. Make a list of the most important facts given in the text. Discuss your findings with your neighbour and prepare a presentation for the whole class (think – pair – share).
2. Find out more about the railroads and their importance in the second half of the 19th century.
3. "Rain follows the plow." Do you think the farmers were just stupid to believe in these "rules" or do ideas like that still exist today?

A model for democracy?

4. In a comment in *Newsweek* ("Democracy: If You Want to Free Your Country, First Liberate Its Land", Sept. 20, 2008) Fareek Zakaria argues that "The 1862 Homestead Act, which gave away 10 percent of the land in the United States, [converted] a backward peasant society into a modern capitalist one, which then creates the basis for civil society and democracy." Compare this thesis to the opinion given in the text.

"Go West" – America, the land of unlimited possibilities

5. Imagine you live in 1870 and are an immigrant from Ireland. You have settled in Oklahoma and filed for land under the Homestead Act. Write to your cousin Patrick and tell him about your life, trying to persuade him to come to America with his family.

# Telegraph Road[1]

Mark Knopfler

Before you read/ listen

Have a close look at the painting (p. 18) again. What is the woman holding in her left hand?

A long time ago came a man on a track
Walking thirty miles with a sack on his back
And he put down his load where he thought it was the best
Made a home in the wilderness
Built a cabin and a winter store

[1] **Telegraph Road** US 24 is known as Telegraph Road. The road was so named due to the telegraph lines running alongside the road for a great distance more than a century ago. Today it is part of the Michigan Highway system.

And he ploughed up the ground by the cold lake shore
The other travellers came walking down the track
And they never went further, no, they never went back
Then came the churches, then came the schools
Then came the lawyers, then came the rules
Then came the trains and the trucks with their loads
And the dirty old track was the telegraph road

Then came the mines, then came the ore[2]
Then there was the hard times then there was a war
Telegraph sang a song about the world outside
Telegraph road got so deep and so wide
Like a rolling river ...

And my radio says tonight it's gonna freeze
People driving home from the factories
There's six lanes of traffic
Three lanes moving slow ...

I used to like to go to work but they shut it down
I got a right to go to work but there's no work here to be found
Yes and they say we're gonna have to pay what's owed
We're gonna have to reap from some seed that's been sowed
And the birds up on the wires and the telegraph poles
They can always fly away from this rain and this cold
You can hear them singing out their telegraph code
All the way down the telegraph road

You know I'd sooner forget but I remember those nights
When life was just a bet on a race between the lights
You had your head on my shoulder you had your hand in my hair
Now you act a little colder like you don't seem to care
But just believe in me baby and I'll take you away
From out of this darkness and into the day
From these rivers of headlights these rivers of rain
From the anger that lives on the streets with these names
'Cos I've run every red light on memory lane[3]
I've seen desperation[4] explode into flames
And I don't want to see it again ...
From all of these signs saying sorry but we're closed
All the way down the telegraph road

**▼ Compare to the steps in Turner's description of development (p. 19 ff.).**

**Mark Knopfler**

**▼ Contrast with the situation at the beginning of the song**

---

[2] **ore** *Erz* [3] **memory lane** (here) general expression for sth. of the past held dearly
[4] **desperation** *Verzweiflung*

## Activities

The story in a song

1. Retell the history/story of Telegraph Road in your own words.
2. The singer (narrator) of the song offers a possibility how to end the misery. Do you think his suggestion is realistic?

Analysing the style

3. Make a list of the most important stylistic devices used in the song. What effect do they create?

4. Mark Knopfler wrote the song travelling along Highway 24 in Michigan. He tried to imagine the history of the road and the settlements from the early times until today. In a project work gather all information you can find about "Telegraph Road". You may illustrate your poster with photos. Use the lyrics of the song as guidance.

A song for Independence Day?

5. "Telegraph Road" is one of the longest songs (14:12 min) in pop history. Therefore it is not often played on the radio. A local radio station has asked for propositions for a special July 4th programme. Write an e-mail giving your reasons why this song should be played.

The "road metaphor" in American history

6. On its western end Telegraph Road is continued by the even more famous Route 66 . Draw a mind map noting ideas as to why roads play such an important role in American popular culture.

# The "New" Frontier: Address at Rice University on the Nation's Space Effort

John F. Kennedy

Before you read

Running for President, John F. Kennedy spoke about the challenge of a "New Frontier", which became the motto of his campaign. In his nomination speech on July 15, 1960 in Los Angeles he said: "[...] we stand today on the edge of a New Frontier – the frontier of the 1960s – a frontier of unknown opportunities and perils – a frontier of unfulfilled hopes and threats. [...] Beyond that frontier are the uncharted areas of science and space [...]." Three years later, the USA still suffering from the "Sputnik shock", he initialized a space programme, which, at the time, not many believed could be fulfilled.

**John F. Kennedy (1917–1963), 35th President**

William Bradford,[1] speaking in 1630 of the founding of the Plymouth Bay Colony, said that all great and honorable actions are accompanied with great difficulties, and both must be enterprised[2] and overcome with answerable[3] courage.

If [the] history of our progress teaches us anything, it is that man, in his quest for knowledge and progress, is determined and cannot be deterred[4]. The exploration of space will go ahead, whether we join in it or not, and it is one of the great adventures of all time, and no nation which expects to be the leader of other nations can expect to stay behind in the race for space. Those who came before us made certain that this country rode the first

**What implications are ▼ hidden in the word "leadership"?**

[1] **William Bradford (1590–1657)** leader and governor of the settlers in Plymouth, Massachusetts [2] **to enterprise** to undertake [3] **answerable** (old use) responsible
[4] **to deter** *abschrecken*

waves of the industrial revolutions, the first waves of modern invention, and the first wave of nuclear power, and this generation does not intend to founder[5] in the backwash[6] of the coming age of space. We mean to be a part of it – we mean to lead it. For the eyes of the world now look into space, to the moon and to the planets beyond, and we have vowed that we shall not see it governed by a hostile flag of conquest, but by a banner of freedom and peace. We have vowed that we shall not see space filled with weapons of mass destruction, but with instruments of knowledge and understanding. Yet the vows of this Nation can only be fulfilled if we in this Nation are first, and, therefore, we intend to be first. In short, our leadership in science and in industry, our hopes for peace and security, our obligations to ourselves as well as others, all require us to make this effort, to solve these mysteries, to solve them for the good of all men, and to become the world's leading space-faring nation.

We set sail on this new sea because there is new knowledge to be gained, and new rights to be won, and they must be won and used for the progress of all people. For space science, like nuclear science and all technology, has no conscience of its own. Whether it will become a force for good or ill depends on man, and only if the United States occupies a position of pre-eminence can we help decide whether this new ocean will be a sea of peace or a new terrifying theater of war. I do not say that we should or will go unprotected against the hostile misuse of space any more than we go unprotected against the hostile use of land or sea, but I do say that space can be explored and mastered without feeding the fires of war, without repeating the mistakes that man has made in extending his writ around this globe of ours.

▼ **Why has he chosen the "sea" metaphor?**

There is no strife, no prejudice, no national conflict in outer space as yet. Its hazards are hostile to us all. Its conquest deserves the best of all mankind, and its opportunity for peaceful cooperation may never come again. But why, some say, the moon? Why choose this as our goal? And they may well ask why climb the highest mountain? Why, 35 years ago, fly the Atlantic? [...] We choose to go to the moon. We choose to go to the moon in this decade and do the other things, not because they are easy, but because they are hard, because that goal will serve to organize and measure the best of our energies and skills, because that challenge is one that we are willing to accept, one we are unwilling to postpone, and one which we intend to win, and the others, too.

▼ **The space race: just another step in the Cold War?**

It is for these reasons that I regard the decision last year to shift our efforts in space from low to high gear as among the most important decisions that will be made during my incumbency in the office of the Presidency. [...]

To be sure, we are behind, and will be behind for some time in manned flight. But we do not intend to stay behind, and in this decade, we shall make up and move ahead. [...]

And finally, the space effort itself, while still in its infancy, has already created a great number of new companies, and tens of thousands of new jobs. Space and related industries are generating new demands in investment and skilled personnel, and this city and this State, and this region, will

**Apollo 11 lift-off**

[5] **to founder** to fail because of a problem; (*for a ship*) to sink [6] **the backwash** the movement of the water after the wave has hit the shore/the beach; the waves caused by a boat moving through the water.

**Which concepts of the old frontier are transferred to the new frontier?** ▶

share greatly in this growth. What was once the furthest outpost on the old frontier of the West will be the furthest outpost on the new frontier of science and space. Houston, your City of Houston, with its Manned Spacecraft Center, will become the heart of a large scientific and engineering community. [...]

**Buzz Aldrin (Apollo 11) on the moon, July 20, 1969**

To be sure, all this costs us all a good deal of money. This year's space budget is three times what it was in January 1961, and it is greater than the space budget of the previous eight years combined. That budget now stands at $5,400 million a year – a staggering sum, though somewhat less than we pay for cigarettes and cigars every year. Space expenditures will soon rise some more, from 40 cents per person per week to more than 50 cents a week for every man, woman and child in the United Stated, for we have given this program a high national priority – even though I realize that this is in some measure an act of faith and vision, for we do not now know what benefits await us. [...]

However, I think we're going to do it, and I think that we must pay what needs to be paid. I don't think we ought to waste any money, but I think we ought to do the job. And this will be done in the decade of the sixties. [...] It will be done during the term of office of some of the people who sit here on this platform. But it will be done. And it will be done before the end of this decade. [...]

Many years ago the great British explorer George Mallory, who was to die on Mount Everest, was asked why did he want to climb it. He said, "Because it is there."

Well, space is there, and we're going to climb it, and the moon and the planets are there, and new hopes for knowledge and peace are there. And, therefore, as we set sail we ask God's blessing on the most hazardous and dangerous and greatest adventure on which man has ever embarked.

## Activities

Frontiers without boundaries?

1. Contrast the old frontier to this new frontier: what do they have in common, what is different?

Why put a man on the moon?

2. Draw a mind map collecting and organising all reasons Kennedy gives for space travel:

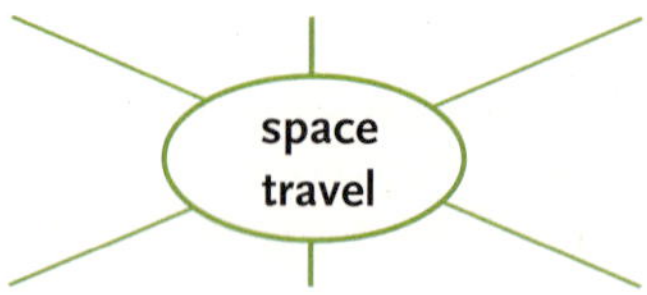


Analysing the speech

3. Examine the rhetorical devices Kennedy employs to convince the audience.

4. In 1962 there were other problems that required a great deal of money. In a hot seat discussion question Kennedy on the space programme.

Promoting the New Frontier

5. As a journalist you have attended the meeting where Kennedy gave this speech. Under the heading "President Kennedy wants every American to spend 50 cents a week for space travel" write an article outlining the main arguments given in the text.

# The American Dream

James Truslow Adams

In a book published just two years after the beginning of the great depression (1929) the American historian and writer J. T. Adams coined the phrase of "the American Dream." He intended a much broader meaning of the phrase than is often used today.

If, as I have said, the things already listed were all we had had to contribute, America would have made no distinctive and unique gift to mankind. But there has been also the American Dream, the dream of a land in which life should be better and richer and fuller for every man, with opportunity for each according to his ability or achievement. It is a difficult dream for the European upper classes to interpret adequately, and too many of us ourselves have grown weary[1] and mistrustful of it. It is not a dream of motor cars and high wages merely, but a dream of a social order in which each man and each woman shall be able to attain to the fullest stature of which they are innately[2] capable, and be recognized by others for what they are, regardless of the fortuitous[3] circumstances of birth or position. [...]

◀ Another Europe – USA comparison: remember the differences Turner pointed out

No, the American dream that has lured[4] tens of millions of all nations to our shores in the past century has not been a dream of merely material plenty, though that has doubtless counted heavily. It has been much more than that. It has been a dream of being able to grow to fullest development as man and woman, unhampered[5] by the barriers which had slowly been erected in older civilizations, unrepressed by social orders which had developed for the benefit of classes rather than for the simple human being of any and every class. And that dream has been realized more fully in actual life here than anywhere else, though very imperfectly even among ourselves. [...]

◀ Is this an adequate definition of "the pursuit of happiness"?

The point is that if we are to have a rich and full life in which all are to share and play their parts, if the American dream is to be a reality, our communal spiritual and intellectual life must be distinctly higher than elsewhere, where classes and groups have their separate interests, habits, markets, arts, and lives. If the dream is not to prove possible of fulfillment, we might as well become stark[6] realists, become once more class-conscious, and struggle as individuals or classes against one another. If it is to come true, those on top, financially, intellectually, or otherwise, have got to devote themselves to the "Great Society," and those who are below in the scale have got to strive[7] to rise, not merely economically, but culturally. We cannot become a great democracy by giving ourselves up as individuals to selfishness, physical comfort, and cheap amusement. The very foundation of the American Dream of a better and richer life for all is that all, in varying degrees, shall be capable of wanting to share in it. It can never be wrought[8] into a reality by cheap people or by "keeping up with the

▼ "Higher than elsewhere"?

---

[1] **to grow weary of sth.** *etwas leid sein* [2] **innately** sth. (usually a quality, ability) you have got when you are born [3] **fortuitous** sth. happening by chance [4] **to lure** to persuade or to trick sb. to go somewhere [5] **unhampered** *unbehindert* [6] **stark** complete, extreme [7] **to strive** to try very hard to achieve sth. [8] **wrought** (old past tense of **to work**) *here* to turn into/to bring

Joneses[9]." There is nothing whatever in a fortune merely in itself or in a man merely in himself. It all depends on what is made of each. Lincoln was not great because he was born in a log cabin[10], but because he got out of it – that is, because he rose above the poverty, ignorance, lack of ambition, shiftlessness of character, contentment with mean things and low aims which kept so many thousands in the huts where they were born.

If we are to make the dream come true we must all work together, no longer to build bigger, but to build better. By working together I do not mean another organization, of which the land is as full as was Kansas of grasshoppers[11]. I mean a genuine individual search and striving for the abiding[12] values of life. In a country as big as America it is as impossible to prophesy as it is to generalize, without being tripped up[13], but it seems to me that there is room for hope as well as mistrust. The epic loses all its glory without the dream. The statistics of size, population, and wealth would mean nothing to me unless I could still believe in the dream. [...]

We have a long and arduous[14] road to travel if we are to realize our American dream in the life of our nation, but if we fail, there is nothing left but the old eternal round[15]. The alternative is the failure of self-government, the failure of the common man to rise to full stature[16], the failure of all that the American dream has held of hope and promise for mankind.

Why does he call ▶ American history an "epic"? Look up the word.

Note the "road" ▶ metaphor.

---

[9] **"keeping up with the Joneses"** a popular catchphrase referring to the desire to be as good, as rich, as wealthy as your neighbours (= the Joneses) [10] **a log cabin** a small house built of wooden beams [11] **grasshoppers** refers to the grasshoppers plague in Kansas at the end of the 19th century (= more than you need) [12] **abiding** lasting, not changing [13] **to be tripped up** to be forced to make a mistake [14] **arduous** involving a lot of effort, difficulty [15] **the old eternal round** a procedure that repeats itself forever [16] **stature** the respect sb. has because of his achievements, ability

## Activities

**The theory of the "Dream"**

1. With your partner make a list of the major elements of the "Dream", as Adams defines them.
2. "If we are to make the dream come true we must all work together, no longer to build bigger, but to build better." (l. 43 f.) Outline the main idea behind this challenge.

**Dream or nightmare?**

3. Gather facts about the economic situation in the USA in 1931. Why would someone write a treatise about "The American Dream" at that time?

**Still a dream for many?**

4. Prepare and stage a debate about the question whether or not America is closer to the attainment of the "Dream".
5. There is a lottery for Green Cards every year. This proves that the "Dream" is still attractive for many people outside the USA. Are you tempted to emigrate to the USA or not? Give reasons.

**The global relevance of the American Dream**

6. Which components of Adam's concept would you adopt as guidelines for a "German Dream"? In groups make a poster and explain your choices.

# Mercedes Benz

Janis Joplin

This political song, written by Janis Joplin (1943–1970) with Michael McClure and Bob Neuwirth, was recorded in just one take three days before she died of an overdose (Oct. 1st, 1970). It is the last song she recorded and so became a sort of final message for many fans.
Following the tradition of early protest songs the song was kept in its rough original form without any further additions (instruments, vocals etc.).

▼ **Keeping up with the Joneses?**

Oh Lord, won't you buy me a Mercedes Benz?
My friends all drive Porsches, I must make amends[1].
Worked hard all my lifetime, no help from my friends,
So Lord, won't you buy me a Mercedes Benz?

Oh Lord, won't you buy me a color TV?
Dialing for Dollars[2] is trying to find me.
I wait for delivery each day until three,
So oh Lord, won't you buy me a color TV?

Oh Lord, won't you buy me a night on the town?
I'm counting on you, Lord, please don't let me down.
Prove that you love me and buy the next round,
Oh Lord, won't you buy me a night on the town?

*(Everybody!)*
Oh Lord, won't you buy me a Mercedes Benz?
My friends all drive Porsches, I must make amends,
Worked hard all my lifetime, no help from my friends,
So oh Lord, won't you buy me a Mercedes Benz?

*(That's it!)*

**Janis Joplin**

---

[1] **to make amends** to improve a situation, to better it [2] **Dialing for Dollars** daytime TV show, where the audience could win a prize, if they answered the phone and gave the right codeword

## Activities

1. List what the singer asks for in each stanza.
2. What type of text does the speaker use to ask for the fulfilment of her demands? Do you think this is adequate?

A dream of motorcars and high wages?

3. What do you think is the intended message of this song?
4. With a partner discuss whether the message of this song is in accordance with Adam's theory of the American Dream.
5. Being responsible for Mercedes Benz advertising in the USA, would you use the song for a radio/television spot? Discuss with a partner and present and justify your decision in class.

A song of great social and political import?

# In the Wake of a Dream

## Immigration from 1850 to 2000 (US Census)

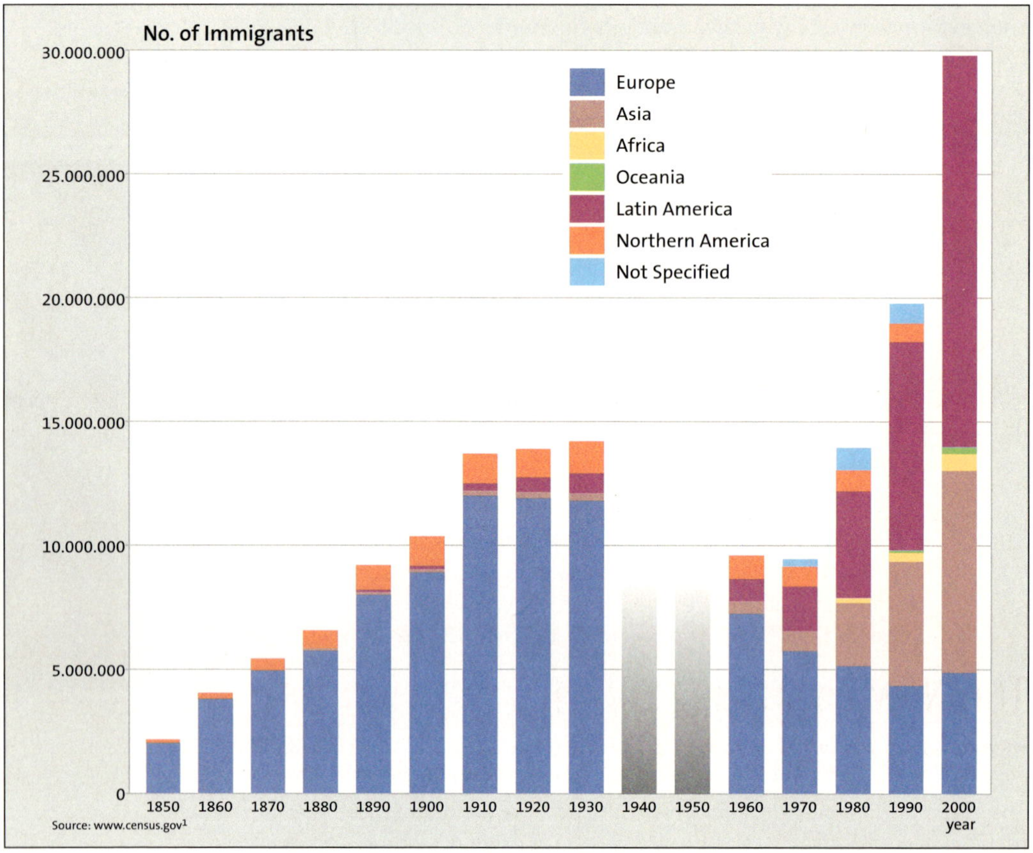


---

[1] There is no official data for 1940 and 1950. Other data show that immigration must have been below 5 000 000.

## Activities

Describing and analysing data

1. Describe the bar chart with regard to the development of immigration from Europe.
2. Analyse the data of immigrants (a) from Asia and (b) from Latin America.
3. Write a short "History of Immigration" using the most important data from this bar chart.

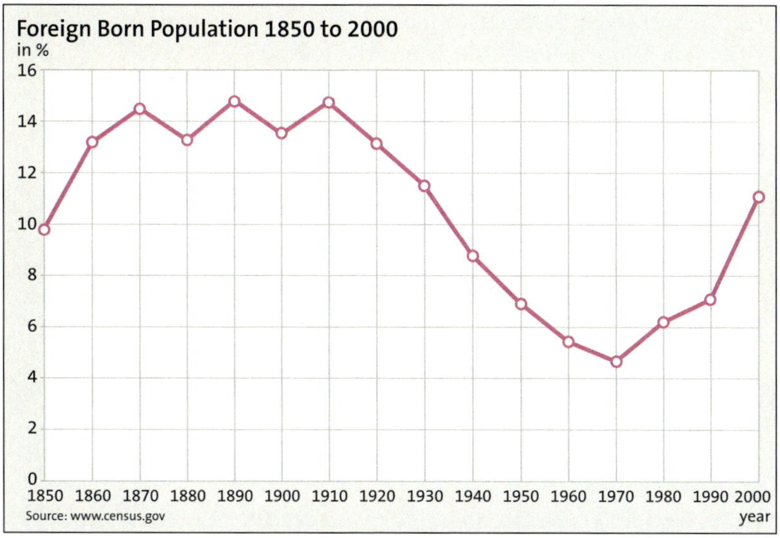


Personalizing graphs

4. Find out how many in your class/group are "foreign born".

Comparing data

5. Compare the graph to the bar chart above. What do they have in common?
6. What may be the implications of the rising figures in the present discussion on "immigration".

# The New Colossus (1883)

Emma Lazarus

The Statue of Liberty was a gift of the French people to the Americans, commemorating the centennial of the Declaration of Independence. The construction of the pedestal took a very long time, as funds ran out of money, so the statue was only finished in 1886. It first served as a lighthouse for New York harbour (till 1902), but meanwhile has become the most prominent icon for the United States worldwide.
Emma Lazarus wrote the poem as a donation to raise funds for the pedestal. It was later engraved on a bronze plaque and mounted in the pedestal of the monument.

Before you read

Find out more about the history of the Statue of Liberty.

Not like the brazen giant of Greek fame,[1]
With conquering limbs astride[2] from land to land;
Here at our sea-washed, sunset gates shall stand
A mighty woman with a torch, whose flame
Is the imprisoned lightning, and her name
Mother of Exiles[3]. From her beacon-hand
Glows world-wide welcome; her mild eyes command
The air-bridged[4] harbor that twin cities frame.

"Keep, ancient lands, your storied pomp[5]!" cries she
With silent lips. "Give me your tired, your poor,
Your huddled masses yearning[6] to breathe free,
The wretched refuse[7] of your teeming shore[8].
Send these, the homeless, tempest-tost[9] to me,
I lift my lamp beside the golden door!"

---

[1] **the brazen giant** the colossus of Rhodes, built about 280 B.C., representing the Sun God [2] **astride** with one leg on each side of sth. [3] **Mother of Exiles** in Jewish tradition *Rachel* is seen as "Mother of Exiles" [4] **air-bridged** reference to the newly built Brooklyn Bridge that connects Manhattan and Brooklyn (twin cities) [5] **storied pomp** (here) old things (i.e. jewellery) used for ceremonies, stored in castles or museums [6] **to yearn** to feel a strong emotional desire; to long for sth. [7] **wretched refuse** (*lit.*) useless things that have been thrown away; (here) people who are not wanted [8] **teeming shore** Europe is seen as overcrowded (compared to the USA) [9] **tost** (old form) tossed; to throw sth. up and down

## Activities

Contrasting the old and new world

**1.** The basic concept of this poem is contrast. Begin by making a list of the things attributed to "old" Europe and those belonging to the "new" world.

| **Old** | **New** |
|---|---|
| – a brazen giant<br>– conquering | – a mighty woman<br>– … |

Comparing form and content

**2.** Analyse the stylistic devices used in the sonnet. How do they underline the message of the poem?

Assuming a different perspective

**3.** The statue was given by the French people to the American people in commemoration of the common republican origins of the Enlightenment (see chapter 1). The poem, written to raise funds for the socket of the statue, was misconstrued interpreting the significance of the statue in a different, even anti-European way. Imagine you were a French citizen reading the poem. Write a letter to the *Statue of Liberty National Monument at National Park Service* responsible for the monument today, stating your (European) point of view.

# E Pluribus Unum – the Motto on the Great Seal of the United States

As an independent country the American nation needed their own national symbols. One of the earliest is the "Great Seal" (1782). You can still find it on every one-dollar bill.

## Activities

1. This picture is taken from a one-dollar bill. Make a list of the symbols you can find. What do they stand for?

Analysing national symbols

2. "E Pluribus Unum" is Latin[1]. It translates "out of many, one." It was adopted as a motto for the Great Seal of the United States in 1782 and first used on a gold coin in 1795 and has since been used on coins and paper bills. Considering your results, what did this motto signify in 1782?

The changing meaning of a national motto

3. Today the motto is often referred to with regard to immigration. How would you translate its meaning in this context?

[1] the words are taken from Virgil's poem "Moretum"

# Ellis Island

Joseph Bruchac

Joseph Bruchac (*1942), author and storyteller lives in the countryside in the state of New York. Though only partly Indian, he dedicates most of his work to the preservation of the Abenaki tribe and cultural heritage.

Before you read

In groups gather all the information you can about Ellis Island. Make a poster using photos and historical information.

Beyond the red brick of Ellis Island
where the two Slovak children
who became my grandparents
waited the long days of quarantine,
after leaving the sickness,
the old Empires of Europe,
a Circle Line ship[1] slips easily
on its way to the island
of the tall woman, green
as dreams of forests and meadows
waiting for those who'd worked
a thousand years
yet never owned their own.

You have come across ▲ these images before

Try to say this in a ► clearer way

Like millions of others,
I too come to this island,
nine decades the answerer
of dreams.

Yet only one part of my blood loves that memory
Another voice speaks
of native lands,
within this nation.
Lands invaded
when the earth became owned.
Lands of those who followed
the changing Moon,
knowledge of the seasons
in their veins.

[1] **Circle Line ship** tourist boat service that cruises round Manhattan

Main building on Ellis Island

## Activities

1. Take evidence from the text and define the origins of the speaker. You may try to sketch a rough family tree.

"E pluribus unum" – detecting an identity

2. The poem consists of four, more or less complex sentences. Nevertheless, there is a number of stylistic devices enhancing the meaning of the text. Make a list of those you think most striking. Compare with your neighbour and agree on a common presentation (think – pair – share).

A closer look at the stylistic devices

3. Analyse the images that express the speaker's divided identity. Which part of his identity do you think predominates?

American Dream and Melting Pot

4. To describe the American nation the metaphor "the melting pot", describing the multicultural American society, is often used. Evaluate the image from the point of view of the speaker of this poem.

# And Lost There, a Golden Feather in a Foreign, Foreign Land

Amy Bloom

**Amy Bloom**

Lillian Leyb travelled to New York from the Belarussian town of Turov, after her family were killed in an anti-Jewish pogrom[1]. She arrives at New York harbour on July 3, 1924.

It had taken eight hours for Lillian to get from Ellis Island to the Battery Park of Manhattan and another four to find Cousin Frieda's apartment building. She had read Cousin Frieda's letter and the directions to Great Jones Street while she stood on three different lines in the Registry Room, while the doctor watched them all climb the stairs, looking for signs of lameness or bad hearts or feeble-mindedness. ("You step lively," a man had said to her on the crossing. "They don't want no idiots in America. Also," and he showed Lillian a card with writing on it, "if you see something that looks like this, scratch your right ear." Lillian tried to memorize the shape of the letters. "What does it say?" "What do you think? It says 'Scratch your right ear.' You do that, they think you can read English. My brother sent me this," the man said and he put the card back in his pocket, like a man with money.)

**▼ Why open a parenthesis here?**

They had room, Cousin Frieda's letter had said, for family or dear friends. They had a little sewing business and could provide employment while people got on their feet. It was a great country, she wrote. Anyone could buy anything – you didn't have to be gentry[2]. There was a list of things Frieda

**▼ The American Dream in a nutshell?**

[1] **pogrom** the organized killing of a large number of people because of their race or/and their religion [2] **gentry** people belonging to a high social class

had bought recently: a sewing machine (on installment[3], but she had it already), white flour in paper sacks, condensed milk, sweet as cream and didn't go bad, Nestle's powdered cocoa for a treat in the evening, hairpins that matched her hair color exactly, very good stockings, only ten cents. They had things here that people in Turov couldn't even imagine.

Lillian had walked through the last door, marked PUSH TO NEW YORK, and showed her letter to a man moving luggage onto the ferry.

**Are these images of a ▼ dream, too?**

He smiled and shrugged[4]. She held up the letter and the block-printed address a dozen times to faces that were blank or, worse than blank, knowing and dubious; she held it up, without much hope, to people who could not themselves read and pushed her aside as if she'd insulted them. She hadn't imagined that in front of her new home, in her new country – after the trolley cars and the men with signs on their fronts and their backs, the women in short skirts, the colored boys with chairs on their backs and pictures of shiny shoes around their necks, and a team, an old man in red pants working with a young girl with a red hat, selling shoelaces, fans, pencils, and salted twists of dough, which smelled so good, Lillian had to cover her mouth and swallow hard – the first thing she would see when she finally got to Great Jones Street was a woman in her nightgown and a man's overcoat, weeping. Lillian watched the woman open a folding chair and take a china plate from her pocket and hold it on her lap. People passed by and put a few coins in the plate.

**A nightmare or just ▼ life?**

Cousin Frieda had run down the stairs and hugged Lillian. "Dear little Lillian," she said. "My home is your home." Frieda was thirty. Lillian remembered her from a family wedding when Frieda took her into the woods and they picked wild raspberries until it was dark. Lillian watched the woman across the street, sitting stock-still in the chair, tears flowing down her face onto her large, loose breasts, dripping onto the plate with the coins.

"Eviction[5]," Frieda said. "You can't pay, you can't stay." She said in Yiddish[6], *"Es iz shver tzu makhen a leben."* It's hard to make a living.

She wanted to make sure Lillian understood. She didn't want Lillian to be frightened, she said, everything would work out fine between them, but Lillian should see, right away, how it's nothing to go from having a home, which Lillian does now, with her cousin Frieda, to having no home at all, like the woman over there who was thrown out this morning. Lillian did see.

Frieda took Lillian by the hand and crossed the street. She put a penny in the plate and said, "I'm sorry, Mrs. Lipkin." Taking Lillian up the stairs to her apartment, Frieda said to Lillian, "Poor thing," and she gestured over her shoulder to a small room filled with a bed and two wooden crates[7]. "You share with Judith."

The lesson of Mrs. Lipkin was not lost on Lillian, still holding everything she had in Yitzak Nirenberg's leather satchel.

---

[3] **installment** payments that are made regularly over a period of time. [4] **to shrug** to raise your shoulders and then drop them to show that you do not know [5] **eviction** to be legally forced to leave your home [6] **Yiddish** a Jewish language spoken in central and eastern Europe, based on a form of German with words from Hebrew and some other European languages [7] **crate** a large wooden container

## Activities

Immigration: a case study

1. Write down the pieces of advice Lillian has to keep in mind while passing through Ellis Island.
2. Complete the list of the things Lillian expected about America and those that surprised her:

| expected | unexpected |
|---|---|
| – anyone can buy anything | – people who can't read |
| – ... | – ... |
| – ... | – ... |

The point of view of a new immigrant

3. Analyse how the point of view contributes to the atmosphere of this passage into a new life.

Discussing the dreams

4. Imagine being Lillian who writes her first impressions into her diary.
5. Enact a dialogue between Frieda and Lillian discussing their hopes and fears. First make notes, but try to act it out freely.

# Republican National Convention Address (2004)

Arnold Schwarzenegger

Arnold Schwarzenegger

Arnold Schwarzenegger was born in Thal, near Graz, in Austria in 1947. His first very successful career as a bodybuilder led him to immigrate to the USA in 1968. He soon began a second career playing in action movies. His breakthrough came with the role of "Conan" in 1982. Later his choice of acting broadened to comedy ("Twins", 1988), too. His political career began in the eighties. Schwarzenegger had supported Ronald Reagan's health programme and registered as a Republican. In a recall election in 2003 he ran for Governor of California. He won and was re-elected in 2006.
Schwarzenegger has been married to Maria Shriver, niece of President John F. Kennedy, since 1986.

Thank you. This is like whining an Oscar. As if I would know! Speaking of acting, one of my movies was called "True Lies." And that's what the Democrats should have called their convention. [...]
Anyway, my fellow Americans, this is an amazing moment for me. To think that a once scrawny boy from Austria could grow up to become Governor of the State of California and then stand here and stand here in Madison Square Garden and speak on behalf of the President of the United States. That is an immigrant's dream! It's the American dream.
You know, I was born in Europe and I've traveled all over the world, and I can tell you that there is no place, no country, that is more compassionate,

◂ Why does he mention his travels?

more generous, more accepting, and more welcoming than the United States of America.

As long as I live – As long as I live, I will never forget the day 21 years ago when I raised my right hand and I took the oath of citizenship. You know how proud I was? I was so proud that I walked around with the American flag around my shoulder all day long.

Tonight, I want to talk to you about why I'm even more proud to be an American – why I am proud to be a Republican, and why I believe that this country is in good hands.

When I was a boy, the Soviets occupied part of Austria. I saw their tanks in the streets. I saw communism with my own eyes. I remember the fear we had when we had to cross into the Soviet sector[1]. Growing up, we were told, "Don't look the soldiers in the eye. Just look straight ahead." It was common belief that the Soviet soldiers could take a man out of his own car and ship him back to the Soviet Union as slave labor.

**Is this true? ▶**

Now my family didn't have a car – but one day we were in my uncle's car. It was near dark as we came to the Soviet checkpoint. I was a little boy. I was not an action hero back then. But I remember – I remember how scared I was that the soldiers would pull my father or my uncle out of the car and I would never see them again. My family and so many others lived in fear of the Soviet boot. Today, the world no longer fears the Soviet Union and it is because of the United States of America!

As a kid – As a kid I saw socialist – the socialist country that Austria became after the Soviets left. Now don't misunderstand me: I love Austria and I love the Austrian people. But I always knew that America was the place for me. In school, when the teacher would talk about America, I would daydream about coming here. I would daydream about living here. I would sit there and watch for hours American movies, transfixed by my heroes, like John Wayne. Everything about America – Everything about America seemed so big to me, so open, so possible.

**Why John Wayne? ▶ Whom would you name as an American stereotype?**

I finally arrived here in 1968. What a special day it was. I remember I arrived here with empty pockets, but full of dreams, full of determination, full of desire. The presidential campaign was in full swing. I remember watching the Nixon and Humphrey presidential race on TV. A friend of mine who spoke German and English translated for me. I heard Humphrey saying things that sounded like socialism, which I had just left. But then I heard Nixon speak. Then I heard Nixon speak. He was talking about free enterprise, getting the government off your back, lowering the taxes and strengthening the military.

Listening to Nixon speak sounded more like a breath of fresh air. I said to my friend, I said, "What party is he?" My friend said, "He's a Republican." I said, "Then I am a Republican." And I have been a Republican ever since! And trust me – And trust me in my wife's family, that's no small achievement[2]. But I am proud to be with the Party of Abraham Lincoln, the Party of Teddy Roosevelt, the Party of Ronald Reagan and the Party of George W. Bush!

To my fellow immigrants listening tonight, I want you to know how wel-

---

[1] **Soviet sector** after the Second World War the Russians occupied the eastern part of Austria until October 1955 [2] Schwarzenegger is married to Maria Shriver, a member of the Kennedy clan (= Democratic Party)

come you are in this party. We Republicans admire your ambition. We encourage your dreams. We believe in you[r] future. And one thing I learned about America is that if you work hard and if you play by the rules, this country is truly open to you. You can achieve anything.

Everything I have – my career, my success, my family – I owe to America. In this country, it doesn't make any difference where you were born. It doesn't make any difference who your parents were. It doesn't make any difference if you're like me and you couldn't even speak English until you were in your twenties.

▼ Is this general statement true?

America gave me opportunities and my immigrant dreams came true. I want other people to get the same chances I did, the same opportunities. And I believe they can. That's why I believe in this country. [...]

Now, many of you out there tonight are "Republican" like me – in your hearts and in your belief. Maybe you're from Guatemala. Maybe you're from the Philippines. Maybe you're from Europe or the Ivory Coast. Maybe you live in Ohio, Pennsylvania, or New Mexico. And maybe – And maybe, just maybe, you don't agree with this Party on every single issue. I say to you tonight that I believe that's not only okay, but that's what's great about this country. Here – Here we can respectfully disagree and still be patriotic, still be American, and still be good Republicans. [...]

You know, when the Germans brought down the Berlin Wall, America's determination helped wield[3] the sledgehammers. And when the lone, young Chinese man stood in front of those tanks in Tiananmen Square, America stood with him. And when Nelson Mandela smiled in election victory after all those years in prison, America celebrated, too.

▼ Do you remember photos of these three historical events?

We are still the lamp lighting the world, especially [for] those who struggle. No matter in what labor camp they slave, no matter in what injustice they're trapped, they hear our call; they see our light; and they feel the pull of our freedom.

◀ What does "the lamp" allude to?

They come here as I did because they believe. They believe in us. They come because their hearts say to them, as mine did, "If only I can get to America." You know, someone once wrote[4]: "There are those who say that freedom is nothing but a dream." They are right. It's the American dream. No matter the nationality, no matter the religion, no matter the ethnic background, America brings out the best in people. And as Governor – as Governor of the great state of California, I see the best in Americans every day – I see the best in Americans everyday – our police, our firefighters, our nurses, doctors, and teachers, our parents.

And what about the extraordinary men and women who have volunteered to fight for the United States of America. I have such great respect for them and their heroic families. [...]

My fellow Americans, I want you to know that I believe with all my heart that America remains "the great idea" that inspires the world. It is a privilege to be born here. It is an honor to become a citizen here. It is a gift to raise your family here, to vote here and to live here. [...]

Thank you, America. Thank you and God bless you all. Thank you. Thank you.

[3] **to wield** to hold sth. and use it as a tool or weapon [4] there is no traceable source for this quotation!

## Activities

Autobiography blended with World History

1. Outline the main elements of this autobiographical text.
2. Make a list of the historical events Arnold Schwarzenegger refers to in his speech.

Dismantling political rhetoric

3. On a poster draw and complete the following clusters:

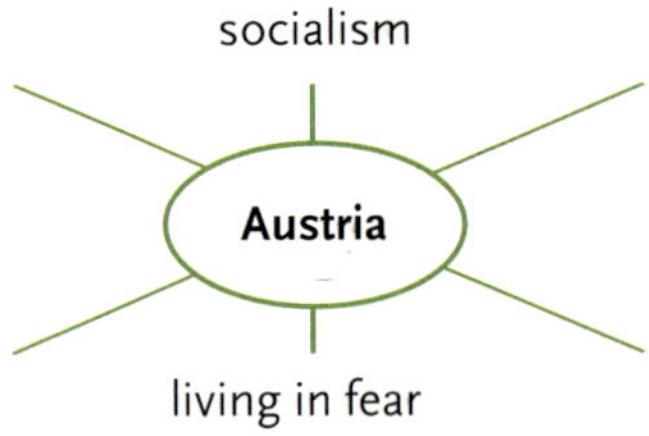


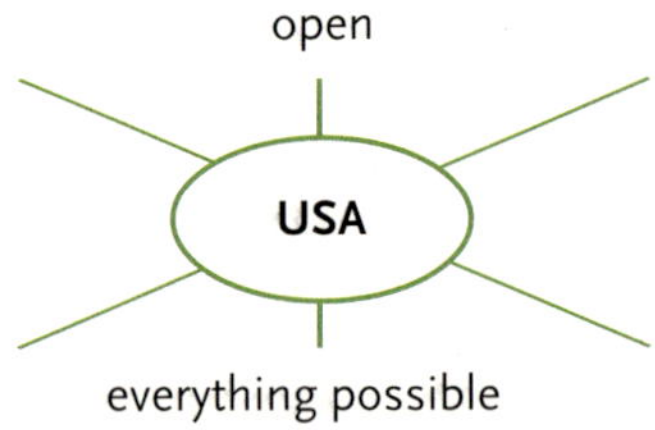


4. Do you think that what Schwarzenegger says about Austria is still relevant? Discuss.
5. Try to write a definition of the "American Dream" as Schwarzenegger sees it.

Planning an interview

6. You are a journalist from a Latin American country. Write an interview with Governor Schwarzenegger reflecting his attitude towards immigration.

# The Tortilla Curtain

T. C. Boyle

T. Coraghessan Boyle is the author of nearly twenty books of fiction. He holds a Ph. D. in English literature and teaches at the English Department of the University of Southern California. *The Tortilla Curtain* was published in 1995. The main topic of the novel is the xenophobia of the Californian middle class facing illegal immigration from Mexico.

Before you read

1. Describe the cartoon.
2. In a dictionary look up the word "borderline". Also check medical use as in "borderline syndrome".
3. Summarize how the cartoonist presents the state of discussion about immigration in the USA.

Delaney Mossbacher is a writer for environmental magazines. With his wife and their child they live in "Piñon Drive" in a Los Angeles neighbourhood called "Arroyo Blanco Estates." The all-white American community has just decided to follow the proposition of their president, Jack Jardine, to shut the estate with a gate. Delaney was against the motion as it hurt his liberal-humanist ideals, but found his arguments turned down by Jack Jardine. Some days later he meets Jack, his lawyer and counselor, at the mall, shopping.

"[...] the gate thing is important, probably the single most important agendum[1] we've taken up in my two years as president."

[...] "You really think so? To me, I say it's unnecessary – and, I don't know, irresponsible somehow."

Jack gave him a quizzical[2] look, "Irresponsible?"

Delaney shifted his burden, milk from the right hand to the left, baguettes under the arm, pasta to his chest. "I don't know. I lean more to the position that we live in a democracy, like the guy in the shorts said at the meeting ... I mean, we all have a stake in things[3], and locking yourself away from the rest of society, how can you justify that?"

◄ Note his three shopping items (and their origin).

"Safety. Self-protection. Prudence. You lock your car, don't you? Your front door?" A cluck of the tongue, a shift from one hip to the other, blue eyes, solid as stone. "Delaney, believe me, I know how you feel. You heard Jack Cherrystone speak to the issue, and nobody's credentials can touch Jack's as far as being liberal is concerned, but this society isn't what it was – and it won't be until we get control of the borders."

▼ Take note of how his argumentation unfolds

The borders. Delaney took an involuntary step backwards, all those dark disordered faces rising up from the street corners and freeway onramps to mob his brain, all of them crying out their human wants through mouths full of rotten teeth. "That's racist, Jack, and you know it."

"Not in the least – it's a question of national sovereignty. Did you know that the U. S. accepted more immigrants last year than all the other countries of the world combined – and that half of them settled in California? And that's legal immigrants, people with skills, money, education. The ones coming in through the Tortilla Curtain down there, those are the ones that are killing us. They're peasants, my friend. No education, no resources, no skills – all they've got to offer is a strong back, and the irony is we need fewer and fewer strong backs every day because we've got robotics and computers and farm machinery that can do the labor of a hundred men at a fraction of the cost." He dropped his hand in dismissal. "It's old news."

[1] **agendum** item to be discussed at a meeting; thing that has to be done [2] **quizzical** questioning [3] **a stake in things** sth. that you want to be successful

Delaney set the milk down on the floor. He was in a hurry [...]. "I can't believe you," he said, and he couldn't seem to control his free arm, waving it in an expanding loop. "Do you realize what you're saying? Immigrants are the lifeblood of this country – we're a nation of immigrants – and neither of us would be standing here today if it wasn't."

"Clichés. There's a point of saturation. Besides which, the Jardines fought in the Revolutionary War – you could hardly call us immigrants."

"Everybody's an immigrant from somewhere. My grandfather came over from Bremen and my grandmother was Irish – does that make me any less a citizen than the Jardines?"

[...] Jack worked a little grit[4] into his voice.

"That's not the point. Times have changed, my friend. Radically. Do you have any idea what these people are costing us, and not just in terms of crime, but in real tax dollars for social services? No? Well, you ought to. You must have seen that thing in the Times[5] a couple weeks ago, about the San Diego study[6]?"

Delaney shook his head. He felt his stomach sink [...].

"Look, Delaney," Jack went on, cool, reasonable, his voice in full song now, "it's a simple equation, so much in, so much out. The illegals in San Diego County contributed seventy million in tax revenues and at the same time they used up two hundred and forty million in services – welfare, emergency care, schooling and the like. You want to pay for that? And for the crime that comes with it? You want another crazy Mexican throwing himself under your wheels hoping for an insurance payoff? Or worse, you want one of them behind the wheel bearing down on you, no insurance, no brakes, no nothing?"

**▲ How do you feel about these arguments?**

---

[4] **grit** determination [5] **the Times** the Los Angeles Times (or *LA Times*), founded in 1881, 3rd largest distributed newspaper in the USA, considered a quality paper, as it won numerous prizes [6] **the San Diego Study** the University of San Diego regularly undertakes many studies in social development; the results, as far as a greater public is concerned, are often reported in the LA Times; an exact reference to which study may be meant, is not possible

Delaney was trying to organize his thoughts. He wanted to tell Jack that he was wrong, that everyone deserved a chance in life and that the Mexicans would assimilate just like the Poles, Italians, Germans, Irish and Chinese and that besides which we'd stolen California from them in the first place, but he didn't get the chance. [...] They were moving in the direction of the cash registers [...] and Jack, the conciliatory Jack, Jack the politician, Jack the soother of gripes[7], grievances and hurts real or imaginary, put an arm over Delaney's shoulder and warbled[8] his sweetest notes: "Listen, Delaney, I know how you feel, and I agree with you. It's not easy for me either – it's nothing less than rethinking your whole life, who you are and what you believe in. And trust me: when we get control of the border again – if we get control of it – I'll be the first to advocate taking that gate down. But don't kid yourself: it's not going to happen anytime soon." [...] "Sorry for the lecture," Jack crooned[9] in his ear. "You see my point though?" [...]
"All right, Jack," he said finally, conceding the field.

---

[7] **gripe** a complaint [8] **to warble** to sing like a bird [9] **to croon** to sing sth. gently

## Activities

1. Summarize in your own words what the discussion between Delaney Mossbacher and Jack Jardine is about.
2. Make two lists: one of Jack Jardine's arguments against immigration and one of Delaney Mossbacher's in favour of immigration.
3. Compare the two opinions to Arnold Schwarzenegger's arguments. Living in California, which of the two might vote for a Governor Schwarzenegger? Give reasons.

The limitations of a dream

4. Analyse the techniques of persuasion Jack uses to convince Delaney.

Detecting techniques of persuasion

5. Stage a panel discussion. Find more arguments for both sides. The motion might read: "We believe that the USA are saturated and immigration to the USA should be stopped."

Preparing a panel discussion

# Migrate, then Integrate

Gregory Rodriguez

Jack Jardine quotes a "San Diego study" from the "Times". The *Los Angeles Times* is the third largest distributed daily newspaper in the United States. It is a quality paper and its authors have won numerous prizes. The following article is taken from the newspaper. The author, Gregory Rodriguez (you may speculate about his origins), is an Op-Ed[1] columnist for the *Los Angeles*

---

[1] **op-ed** an 'op-ed' is "opposite the editorial page"; this is usually an article (opinion) written by a named author not affiliated to the staff of the newspaper/magazine

*Times*. He is Director of the California Fellows Program and a well known writer who has published several studies on immigration. The following article refers to recent data about the change in immigration.

It's too bad Congress is still stuck on the issue of immigration because, here in Los Angeles, we're getting ready to move on to bigger and perhaps better things: the rise of the post-immigrant population.

Back in February, a USC[2] study reported that Los Angeles County had seen a 30% drop in new immigrant arrivals in the 1990s. In March, the Urban Institute released a report showing that even as the nation at large experienced an increase in its undocumented population between 2002 and 2004, L.A. actually lost roughly 15,000 illegal immigrants. And now the Census Bureau's 2005 American Community Survey tells us that, for the first time since at least 1960, the foreign-born percentage of Los Angeles residents is going down.

Compare to the graph ▶ on p. 33.

In the first half of this decade, according to census estimates, the percentage of L.A. County residents who were born outside the U.S. dropped from 36.2% to 36.0%. In the city, that figure declined from 40.9% to 40.3%. No, the percentage slip isn't enormous, but its historical significance for our region could not be greater. It signals the emergence[3] of an era in which integration will become a significantly more important issue than immigration.

Remember where ▶ Lillian Leyb went to when she first arrived in New York (cf. p. 37).

Consider the demographic trends of the last half a century. Since 1960, newcomers have become an ever-increasing portion of the population. In L.A., the number of foreignborn residents grew by an average of 50% every decade. In the 1970s, the growth rate reached a phenomenal 96%. This means that, as the city grew, it also fractured. Newcomers, many of them undocumented, had a tenuous toehold[4] in U.S. society and generally sought comfort among their own. As has happened throughout U.S. history, late-20th century immigrants sought to re-create the sounds and smells and networks of home in their new land. The once highly homogenous City of Angels became increasingly divided along not just racial but cultural and linguistic lines. In their attempt to respond to this growing diversity, government, business and the media came to perceive Los Angeles as a confederation of isolated, self-sustaining ethnic enclaves. The idea of integration was trumped[5] by the need for outreach[6]. At the time, it made sense. To navigate this amazing diversity, entities[7] from social service agencies to bank marketing divisions developed separate, linguistically and culturally unique appeals[8] targeting an array[9] of distinct "communities." The target audience within those communities was generally foreignborn householders who had arrived in the U.S. within a decade or two.

Particularly vis-a-vis the growing Latino population, many mediating[10] civic organizations that had once sought to include Angelenos[11] of many back-

---

[2] **USC** United States Census [3] **emergence** sth. that comes into being [4] **tenuous toehold** very weak and fragile base [5] **to trump** (in card games) to play a card that beats another card [6] **outreach** *Hilfe/Unterstützung* [7] **entity** *selbständige/unabhängige Organisationen/Gruppierungen* [8] **appeal** an offer [9] **array** an impressive display [10] **to mediate** to establish a common ground between two different communities/groups [11] **Angelenos** Hispanic inhabitants of Los Angeles

grounds now preferred to set up separate "Latino programs" and programming. Because immigration was driving Latino population growth, "Latino outreach" began to be conducted with the cultural practices of foreign-born adults in mind. For example, rather than expanding its appeal to U. S.-born, English-speaking Latinos, local public television station KCET chose to put a Spanish-language program on the air. Likewise, even as many newspapers began to publish Spanish-language editions, their commitment to including English-dominant Latinos in their staffs and stories flagged[12].

▼ **Compare to the situation in Germany; consider TV programmes, for example.**

But with the immigrant portion of the population in decline, this way of understanding and approaching diversity in our city is quickly becoming outdated. This doesn't mean that the region's ethnic metamorphosis is over, but simply that it will be less immigrant-driven. Indeed, this demographic shift is hastening the arrival of the moment that every migration experiences, when the U. S.-born children of immigrants begin to eclipse[13] their parents.

◀ **Do you perceive the same development in Germany's foreign-born population?**

Often bilingual, this second generation tends to play the role of mediators for the first. While less-educated immigrants can spend their lives acclimating to this country, the second generation actively negotiates the gap between their parents' home culture and the American mainstream. Raised on Britney and Buffy and schooled in English, it is this cohort that begins to go beyond the cultural enclave. They are not immigrants but ethnic Americans. And for all the talk of trans-nationalism, they wouldn't quite fit back in Sinaloa[14], Uttar Pradesh[15] or Surat Thani[16].

In other words, if the second generation that is coming of age today is anything like previous children of immigrants, they will not settle for outreach but will increasingly demand full inclusion in their country of birth. This will require us all to develop a more holistic notion of diversity, one that incorporates rather than segregates difference and emphasizes cross-ethnic ties over group-specific appeals.

The rise of the second generation should remind us that "community" doesn't just refer to ethnic and other minority groups but to the people who live together in any given geographic location. It is a sense of solidarity and common purpose among neighbors that we now have a greater chance to rebuild.

◀ **Reconsider the implications of the Declaration of Independence.**

---

[12] **to flag** (here) *erlahmen* [13] **to eclipse** (here) *in den Hintergrund drängen* [14] **Sinaloa** one of the 31 Mexican states [15] **Uttar Pradesh** Indian state [16] **Surat Thani** largest of the southern provinces of Thailand

## Activities

Outlining the main information in a newspaper article

1. Structure the text and give appropriate headlines.
2. Summarize the most important pieces of information of this article on a poster: use two columns, one labeled 1st generation, the other 2nd generation.
3. Look up the word "community" in a monolingual dictionary. Compare to the definition given by the author in the last paragraph of his article.

Analysing a newspaper article

4. Examine the style of the article and point out which elements show you that this is an argumentative text.

Writing a letter to the editor

5. Imagine you are Delaney Mossbacher and you have just read the article in the *LA Times*. Write a letter to the editor stating your opinion on the subject.

John McCain

# Border Security and Immigration Reform

John McCain

John McCain was the Presidential candidate of the Republican party in the election 2008. One of the early topics of his campaign was immigration.

I have always believed that our border must be secure and that the federal government has utterly failed in its responsibility to ensure that it is secure. If we have learned anything from the recent immigration debate, it is that Americans have little trust that their government will honor a pledge to do the things necessary to make the border secure.

As president, I will secure the border. I will restore the trust Americans should have in the basic competency of their government. A secure border is an essential element of our national security. Tight border security includes not just the entry and exit of people, but also the effective screening of cargo at our ports and other points of entry.

But a secure border will contribute to addressing our immigration problem most effectively if we also:

- Recognize the importance of building strong allies in Mexico and Latin America who reject the siren call of authoritarians like Hugo Chavez, support freedom and democracy, and seek strong domestic economies with abundant economic opportunities for their citizens.

What does this have to do with immigration? ▶

- Recognize the importance of pro-growth policies[1] – keeping government spending in check[2], holding down taxes, and cutting unnecessary regulatory burdens – so American businesses can hire and pay the best.

Does this remind you of the cartoon (p. 42)? ▶

- Recognize the importance of a flexible labor market to keep employers in business and our economy on top. It should provide skilled Americans and immigrants with opportunity. Our education system should ensure skills for our younger workers, and our retraining and assistance programs for displaced[3] workers must be modernized so they can pursue those opportunities.

Migrate, then assimilate? ▶

- Recognize the importance of assimilation of our immigrant population, which includes learning English, American history and civics[4], and respecting the values of a democratic society.

---

[1] **pro-growth policies** the basic ideas are that economic growth occurs when people work more, save more, and invest more. [2] **in check** in control (i.e. not letting them rise)
[3] **displaced workers** (euphemism) workers that have lost their job [4] **civics** (AmE) a school subject that informs how government works and teaches the rights and duties of a citizen

- Recognize that America will always be that "shining city upon a hill[5]," a beacon of hope and opportunity for those seeking a better life built on hard work and optimism.

Border security and our failed immigration system are more examples of an ailing[6] Washington culture in need of reform to regain the trust of Americans. In too many areas – from immigration and pork barrel spending[7] to Social Security, health care, energy security and tax relief – business-as-usual politics prevents addressing the important challenges facing our nation.

---

[5] **shining city upon the hill** the whole phrase is a slightly modified quote of Ronald Reagan's farewell address to the nation (January 11, 1989), based itself on the image given in the "Sermon on the Mount" (Matthew 5:14–16) [6] **ailing** ill/sick and not improving
[7] **pork barrel spending** giving away a lot of money to win votes

## Activities

1. Make a list of the measures concerning immigration John McCain wants to implement if he is elected president.

   *A politician's arguments*

2. Would either Delaney Mossbacher or Jack Jardine (or both) vote for him? Give reasons.

   *Who is his target group?*

3. Schwarzenegger and McCain are members of the same political party (Republican). Which ideas do they share and where do they differ?

   *Same party – different attitudes?*

4. Under the heading "The shining city upon a hill" stage a hot chair discussion questioning John McCain on his attitude towards immigration and the promise of the American Dream.

   *A hot chair discussion*

# A Dream Deferred

Cover of the first edition, 1939

## The Grapes of Wrath

John Steinbeck

During the great depression in the thirties of the last century farmers in the Midwest suffered even more because of a long period of drought destroying the crops. Furthermore, the rapid development of modern agricultural techniques, especially the use of tractors, caused unemployment and favoured industrial farming instead of small family-run farms. The text is taken from the beginning of Steinbeck's novel, published in 1939, which tells the story of the Joad family, pushed from their old farm and daring a long unhappy journey to the west.

At noon the tractor driver stopped sometimes near a tenant[1] house and opened his lunch; sandwiches wrapped in waxed paper, white bread, pickle, cheese, Spam[2], a piece of pie branded like an engine part. He ate without relish[3]. And tenants not yet moved away came out to see him, looked curiously while the goggles[4] were taken off, and the rubber dust-mask, leaving white circles around the eyes and a large white circle around nose and mouth. The exhaust of the tractor puttered on[5], for fuel is so cheap it is more efficient to leave the engine running than to heat the Diesel nose for a new start. Curious children crowded close, ragged children who ate their fried dough as they watched. They watched hungrily the unwrapping of the sandwiches, and their hunger-sharpened noses smelled the pickle, cheese, and Spam. They didn't speak to the driver. They watched his hand as it carried food to his mouth. They did not watch him chewing; their eyes followed the hand that held the sandwich. After a while the tenant who could not leave the place came out and squatted in the shade beside the tractor.

"Why, you're Joe Davis's boy!"

"Sure," the driver said.

"Well, what you doing this kind of work for – against your own people?"

"Three dollars a day. I got damn sick of creeping for my dinner – and not getting it. I got a wife and kids. We got to eat. Three dollars a day, and it comes every day."

"That's right," the tenant said. "But for your three dollars a day fifteen or twenty families can't eat at all. Nearly a hundred people have to go out and wander on the roads for your three dollars a day. Is that right?"

And the driver said: "Can't think of that. Got to think of my own kids. Three dollars a day, and it comes every day. Times are changing, mister, don't you know? Can't make a living on the land unless you've got two, five, ten thousand acres and a tractor. Crop land[6] isn't for little guys like us any more. You

**What does the driver ► compare farming to?**

---

[1] **tenant** sb. who pays rent for a house or land [2] **Spam** finely chopped cooked meat pressed together in a tin [3] **relish** great pleasure [4] **goggles** a pair of glasses that fit closely, made to protect the eyes [5] **to putter on** *weitertuckern* [6] **crop land** *Ackerland*

don't kick up a howl because you can't make Fords, or because you're not the telephone company. Well, crops are like that now. Nothing to do about it. You try to get three dollars a day some place. That's the only way."

The tenant pondered[7]. "Funny thing how it is. If a man owns a little property, that property is him, it's part of him, and it's like him. If he owns property only so he can walk on it and handle it and be sad when it isn't doing well and feel fine when the rain falls on it, that property is him, and some way he's bigger because he owns it. Even if he isn't successful he's big with his property. That is so."

And the tenant pondered more. "But let a man get property he doesn't see, or can't take time to get his fingers in, or can't be there to walk on it – why, then the property is the man. He can't do what he wants, he can't think what he wants. The property is the man, stronger than he is. And he is small, not big. Only his possessions are big – and he's the servant of his property. That is so, too."

The driver munched the branded pie and threw the crust away. "Times are changed, don't you know? Thinking about stuff like that don't feed the kids. Get your three dollars a day, feed your kids. You got no call to worry about anybody's kids but your own. You get a reputation for talking like that, and you'll never get three dollars a day. Big shots won't give you three dollars a day if you worry about anything but your three dollars a day."

"Nearly a hundred people on the road for your three dollars. Where will we go?"

"And that reminds me," the driver said, "you better get out soon. I'm going through the door-yard[8] after dinner."

"You filled in the well[9] this morning."

"I know. Had to keep the line straight. But I'm going through the door-yard after dinner. Got to keep the lines straight. And – well, you know Joe Davis, my old man, so I'll tell you this. I got orders wherever there's a family not moved out – if I have an accident – you know, get too close and cave the house in[10] a little – well, I might get a couple of dollars. And my youngest kid never had no shoes yet."

"I built it with my hands. Straightened old nails to put the sheathing[11] on. Rafters[12] are wired to the stringers[13] with baling wire. It's mine. I built it. You bump it down – I'll be in the window with a rifle. You even come too close and I'll pot[14] you like a rabbit."

**▼ Note the frequent use of the "will future".**

"It's not me. There's nothing I can do. I'll lose my job if I don't do it. And look – suppose you kill me? They'll just hang you, but long before you're hung there'll be another guy on the tractor, and he'll bump the house down. You're not killing the right guy."

---

[7] **to ponder** to think; to consider [8] **door-yard** the yard in front of the door of a house
[9] **to fill in a well** *einen Brunnen zuschütten* [10] **to cave in** the fact of suddenly collapsing
[11] **sheathing** covering; metal protection on a roof [12] **rafters** *Dachsparren* [13] **stringers** *Längsbalken; Pfetten* [14] **to pot** *abknallen*

**Who is responsible? ▼**

"That's so," the tenant said. "Who gave you orders ? I'll go after him. He's the one to kill."

"You're wrong. He got his orders from the bank. The bank told him: 'Clear those people out or it's your job.'"

"Well, there's a president of the bank. There's a board of directors. I'll fill up the magazine of the rifle and go into the bank."

The driver said: "Fellow was telling me the bank gets orders from the east. The orders were: 'Make the land show profit or we'll close you up.'"

"But where does it stop? Who can we shoot? I don't aim to starve to death before I kill the man that's starving me."

"I don't know. Maybe there's nobody to shoot. Maybe the thing isn't men at all. Maybe, like you said, the property's doing it. Anyway, I told you my orders."

"I got to figure[15]," the tenant said. "We all got to figure. There's some way to stop this. It's not like lightning or earthquakes. We've got a bad thing made by men, and by God that's something we can change."

**The tractor = 'he'? ►**

**What does this ► description of the driver remind you of?**

The tenant sat in his doorway, and the driver thundered his engine and started off, tracks falling and curving, harrows[16] combing, and the phalli of the seeder slipping into the ground. Across the door-yard the tractor cut, and the hard, foot-beaten ground was seeded field, and the tractor cut through again; the uncut space was ten feet wide. And back he came. The iron guard bit into the house-corner, crumbled the wall, and wrenched the little house from its foundation so that it fell sideways, crushed like a bug. And the driver was goggled and a rubber mask covered his nose and mouth. The tractor cut a straight line on, and the air and the ground vibrated with its thunder. The tenant man stared after it, his rifle in his hand. His wife was beside him, and the quiet children behind. And all of them stared after the tractor.

[15] **to figure** (here) to think  [16] **harrow** *Egge*

## Activities

1. Write a short summary of the excerpt. Remember to use a neutral style.
2. "Who can we shoot?" Who is responsible for the situation? Draw a pyramid of responsibility, starting with the driver at the bottom.

Summarizing elements of a narrative text

3. Build a freeze frame of the children watching the driver.
4. Back home, the driver tells his wife about the argument with the tenant. Retell from his point of view.
5. Stage a panel discussion between the tenants and the new owners. First, in groups, collect arguments for or against industrial farming. Then choose two speakers for each side.

Taking different views

6. Imagine you are a journalist working for a newspaper on the East Coast. Write a comment on what is going on in the Midwest. Don't forget to make your opinion clear.
7. The conflict between traditional and industrial farming is still relevant today. Gather information about the present situation.

Analysing economic problems past and present

# The Ghost of Tom Joad

Bruce Springsteen

Before you read/ listen

Tom Joad is the protagonist in Steinbeck's *Grapes of Wrath*. On their difficult journey from Oklahoma to California he continues to fight against injustice and brutality. At the end, he revenges the murder of a friend and has to flee. Leaving his family, his mother asks him "How'm I gonna know 'bout you." And his answer is:
"[...] I'll be all aroun' in the dark. I'll be ever'where – wherever you look. Wherever they's a fight so hungry people can eat, I'll be there. Wherever they's a cop beatin' up a guy, I'll be there. [...] I'll be in the way guys yell when they're mad an' – I'll be in the way kids laugh when they're hungry an' they know supper's ready. An' when our folks eat the stuff they raise an' live in the houses they build – why, I'll be there." (Steinbeck, *Grapes of Wrath*)
In the popular culture of the USA, Tom Joad has become "the common man" of the Great Depression. In 1940, after having watched the movie *Grapes of Wrath*, folk singer Woody Guthrie wrote a song about him (*The Ballad of Tom Joad*). Springsteen took up the idea in his song.

Search the Internet for references to *Tom Joad*. What does this character stand for? Quote/Present examples.

**Bruce Springsteen**

Men walkin' 'long the railroad tracks
Goin' someplace and there's no goin' back
Highway patrol choppers comin' up over the ridge

Hot soup on a campfire under the bridge
Shelter line stretchin' round the corner
Welcome to the new world order
Families sleepin' in their cars in the southwest
No home no job no peace no rest

The highway is alive tonight
But nobody's kiddin' nobody[1] about where it goes
I'm sittin' down here in the campfire light
Searchin' for the ghost of Tom Joad

He pulls prayer book out of his sleeping bag
Preacher lights up a butt[2] and takes a drag
Waitin' for when the last shall be first and the first shall be last[3]

In a cardboard box, 'neath the underpass
Got a one-way ticket to the promised land
You got a hole in your belly and gun in your hand
Sleeping on a pillow of solid rock
Bathin' in the city aqueduct

The highway is alive tonight
But where it's headed everybody knows
I'm sittin' down here in the campfire light
Waitin' on the ghost of Tom Joad

Now Tom said "Mom, wherever there's a cop beatin' a guy
Wherever a hungry newborn baby cries
Where there's a fight 'gainst the blood and hatred in the air
Look for me Mom I'll be there
Wherever there's somebody fightin' for a place to stand
Or a decent job or a helpin' hand
Wherever somebody's strugglin' to be free
Look in their eyes Mom you'll see me."

The highway is alive tonight
But nobody's kiddin' nobody about where it goes
I'm sittin' down here in the campfire light
With the ghost of old Tom Joad

---

[1] **nobody is kidding nobody** *niemand macht sich etwas vor* [2] **butt** (slang) a cigarette
[3] quote from the Bible, *Matthew* 19:30 and *Luke* 13:30

## Activities

What does the singer say?

1. Outline what the speaker depicts in the first and second stanza.
2. How does he describe his own situation?
3. Compare the text from Steinbeck's novel and the message of the third stanza. What do they have in common, where do they differ?

4. In groups make a collage (use newspapers/magazines) of the pictures evoked by this song. In a gallery walk explain to the others in your class what your collage shows.

Illustrating a song

5. As an exchange student you have, on your way to California, come across this band of people. Write a letter to your friends back home and tell them about your impressions.

Intercultural reflections

6. Do you know any German pop/rock songs that treat a similar topic?

# A Divided Society

Daniel J. Kevles

The seventies mark the end of the War in Vietnam. The turbulences of the sixties were over and the American society settled to a quieter path. Nevertheless, the social divisions split the population further. The seventies were the decade of the lowest affluence from other countries to the USA (see above, Chapter 3). The following text is taken from an American history book. The author, Daniel J. Kevles is Professor of History at Yale University. Some of the questions raised in the text, are still of present interest.

During the 1970s, the programs and protections deriving from the sixties – the civil rights laws, affirmative action[1], and court decisions – helped change the condition of a growing number of ethnic and racial minority group members. So did their new pride, their unleashed[2] ambition, and a greater tolerance on the part of the white majority. In 1963, half of whites who were asked if they would object to a family member's bringing a black person home to dinner said yes; in 1982 fewer than a quarter did. About the same time 80 percent of whites said they would support a well-qualified black candidate for president, a sharp reversal from the late 1950s, when two-thirds said they

**◀ How does your family feel about bringing members of other ethnic groups home?**

[1] **affirmative action** policies aimed to support or help a minority group [2] **to unleash** to suddenly let a strong feeling/emotion be felt

would not. In these changing circumstances, a rising number of minority-group members made their way in American society, attending college, obtaining better jobs, moving to better neighborhoods. But many were left behind, partly because of discrimination, partly because of the era's economic difficulties. In greater or lesser degree, Americans of color grew increasingly divided among themselves between a burgeoning[3] middle class and a deprived, impoverished lower one. The divide between people of color and the white majority also continued, exacerbated[4] not only by the weakness of the economy but also by a rising tide of immigration.

Between 1959 and 1969, the fraction of blacks living in poverty had fallen from a little more than half to a little less than one-third. In 1970, one out of four blacks was in a middle-class occupation, almost double the number a decade earlier, and at the end of the seventies the number of blacks attending college reached 27 percent, up from 5 percent in 1965. In 1975, eighteen blacks were serving in Congress, including several from the South, more than triple the number in 1965, all of whom had been from the North. During roughly the same period, the number of black elected officials in the South shot up tenfold, with the trend producing a black mayor of Atlanta, one of the South's principal cities.

**Do you think this ► might be a subjective perception?**

Still, faced with white ambivalence[5] and resistance, African Americans were growing more pessimistic about their prospects. The percentage of blacks who perceived discrimination in the workplace increased steadily. In 1976, only 32 percent said that their position in American society had been marked by "real change," a sharp drop from the 60 percent who had agreed with that view in 1964. Racism and discrimination remained realities; so did poverty along the dusty back roads of the South and, especially, in the ghettos of the North, where the decline of the smokestack industries[6] had a disproportionately high impact on unskilled labor.

Poverty was now mainly metropolitan and nonwhite. Although the national poverty rate hovered between 7 and 8 percent during the seventies (down sharply from more than 12 percent in 1965), in the inner cities it increased by 30 percent. The number of people in the impoverished underclass more than doubled in Philadelphia and Chicago; in New York, it almost tripled. Part of it was accounted for by single mothers whose children were not supported by their fathers.

The fraction of unemployed nonwhite males who were neither in school nor in the military shot up from 10 percent in 1964 to more than 25 percent in 1980. The inner cities were pervaded[7] by violent crime and the use of drugs like cocaine. Depending on their age, the murder rate for black males between fifteen and forty-four was between eight and fourteen times higher than the national murder rate, itself the highest in the industrial world.

---

[3] **burgeoning** to grow rapidly [4] **to exacerbate** to make sth. worse [5] **ambivalence** having mixed feelings about sth. [6] **smokestack industries** industries that need chimneys
[7] **to pervade** to be noticeable in every part of sth.

## Activities

1. There is a lot of data in this text from a history book. Structure the text into topical units and then, in groups, draw charts visualizing the data. Give appropriate headings.
2. Discuss the title of the text. Do your charts support this title?
3. Make a double list of things that have improved since the 1950s/60s and those that have worsened.

Organizing and interpreting written data

Evaluating the Dream

# Harlem

Langston Hughes

Langston Hughes (1902–1967) called himself a "black writer", offensively naming the difference. He became well known in the late 1920s and is considered one of the leading Afro-American writers. Born in Missouri, he moved to New York City and spent a lot of his lifetime in Harlem. The house in Harlem he lived in has been given National Landmark status.

Before you read

The stamp was published to commemorate his 100th birthday in 2002. What does this tell you about the author and his importance today?

US postal service, 2002

What happens to a dream deferred[1]?
Does it dry up?
Like a raisin in the sun?
Or fester[2] like a sore –
And then run?
Does it stink like rotten meat
Or crust and sugar over –
Like a syrupy sweet?

Maybe it just sags[3]
Like a heavy load.

*Or does it explode?*

---

[1] **to defer** to delay sth. until a later time [2] **to fester** to become infected [3] **to sag** to hang down

## Activities

Analysing modern poetry

1. In a first step, read the poem silently and try to understand its meaning. Then read it aloud to your class. Compare different presentations.
2. In a few sentences, try to say what the poem is about.

3. Make a list of the most striking stylistic devices. Name the main differences between the first (ll. 1–8), the second (ll. 9–10) and the last (l. 11) stanza.

The message behind the text

4. In groups write down the images of the poem on a poster. You may try to illustrate them with a drawing or a picture. What do they symbolize?

5. The last line/stanza is in different print. Do you think that it contains a warning or a menace? Give reasons.

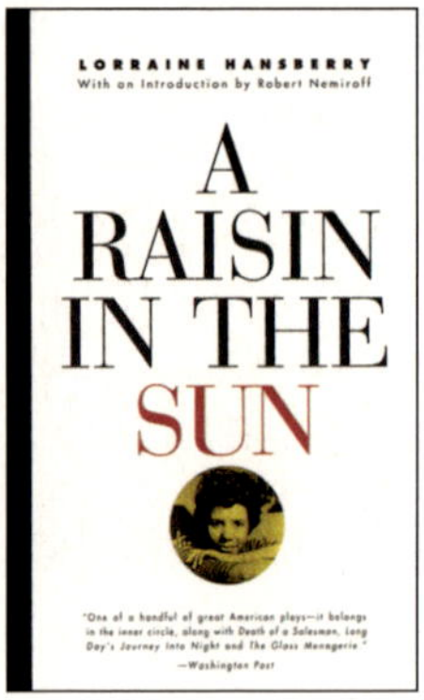


## A Raisin in the Sun

Lorraine Hansberry

Lorraine Hansberry (1930–1965) was born and lived in Chicago. Her play "A Raisin in the Sun", partially based on her own family history, was the first play by a female Afro-American playwright to be played on Broadway. The play was turned into a movie in 1961, starring Sidney Poitier as Walter Lee Younger.

The scene: Joseph Asagai, a student from Nigeria is dating Beneatha Younger, who wants to become a doctor. She is flattered by his advances, but cannot decide to marry him and go back to Africa with him. The Younger family has just found out they have lost a large sum of money, set aside for Beneatha's studies, through a risky venture by her brother Walter Lee Younger.

Think of the ► implications of this metaphor. Is it a good choice?

BENEATHA I know that's what you think. Because you are still where I left off. You with all your talk and dreams about Africa! You still think you can patch up the world. Cure the Great Sore of Colonialism – (*Loftily, mocking it*) with the Penicillin of Independence –!

ASAGAI[1] Yes!

BENEATHA Independence *and then what?* What about all the crooks and thieves and just plain idiots who will come into power and steal and plunder the same as before – only now they will be black and do it in the name of the new Independence – WHAT ABOUT THEM?!

ASAGAI That will be the problem for another time. First we must get there.

BENEATHA And where does it end?

ASAGAI End? Who even spoke of an end? To life? To living?

BENEATHA An end to misery! To stupidity! Don't you see there isn't any real progress, Asagai, there is only one large circle that we march in, around and around, each of us with our own little picture in front of us – our own little mirage that we think is the future.

ASAGAI That is the mistake.

BENEATHA What?

---

[1] **Asagai** taken from *assegai*, a short-handled stabbing spear, common in many parts of Africa

ASAGAI What you just said about the circle. It isn't a circle – it is simply a long line – as in geometry, you know, one that reaches into infinity. And because we cannot see the end – we also cannot see how it changes. And it is very odd but those who see the changes – who dream, who will not give up – are called idealists ... and those who see only the circle we call *them* the "realists"!

BENEATHA Asagai while I was sleeping in that bed in there people went out and took the future right out of my hands! And nobody asked me, nobody consulted me – they just went out and changed my life!

ASAGAI Was it your money?

BENEATHA What?

ASAGAI Was it your money he gave away?

BENEATHA It belonged to all of us.

ASAGAI But did you earn it? Would you have had it at all if your father had not died?

BENEATHA No.

ASAGAI Then isn't there something wrong in a house – in a world – where all dreams, good or bad, must depend on the death of a man? I never thought to see *you* like this, Alaiyo[2]. You! Your brother made a mistake and you are grateful to him so that now you can give up the ailing human race on account of it! You talk about what good is struggle, what good is anything! Where are we all going and why are we bothering!

◀ **Why does he choose to use that nickname and the African dialect?**

---

[2] **Alaiyo** (a nickname; from Yoruba, a Nigerian tribal language) "one for whom bread is not enough"

## Activities

Comparing dreams

1. Apparently Beneatha has lost all hopes and dreams. In your own words sum up her view of life.
2. Asagai has an "African Dream". This dream is partly linked to ideas of the American Dream. Outline the main aspects of his dream.

Verifying the reality of dreams

3. Beneatha criticizes his dream and predicts that the only change will be that the crooks will be black instead of white (see l. 6 ff.). Has she been right or wrong? Check for Nigeria, the country he wants to return to, that became independent in 1960, just one year after the publication of the play.
4. Asagai questions the "dreams, good or bad" of the Younger family. What seems to be the main trait of their dreams?
5. Asagai has been asked by a group of black students to talk about "The African Dream" in contrast to "The American Dream". Write down his main points and try to stage a presentation of his speech. You may add a discussion afterwards.

# I Have Been to the Mountain Top (April 3, 1968)

Martin Luther King

Before you read

This is the last speech given by Martin Luther King. In groups search the main elements of his biography and draw a poster showing the main steps of his political career. What was the political situation in the USA in the spring of 1968 like?

**Martin Luther King**

**Allusion to whom? ▸**

I'm delighted to see each of you here tonight in spite of a storm warning. You reveal that you are determined to go on anyhow. Something is happening in Memphis, something is happening in our world.
As you know, if I were standing at the beginning of time, with the possibility of general and panoramic view of the whole human history up to now, and the Almighty said to me, "Martin Luther King, which age would you like to live in?" – I would take my mental flight by Egypt through, or rather across the Red Sea, through the wilderness on toward the promised land. And in spite of its magnificence, I wouldn't stop there. [...] I would come on up even to 1863, and watch a vacillating[1] president by the name of Abraham Lincoln finally come to the conclusion that he had to sign the Emancipation Proclamation[2]. But I wouldn't stop there. I would even come up to the early

[1] **vacillating** to change one's opinion very often [2] **Emancipation Declaration** issued in September 1862 it declared the freedom of all American slaves

thirties, and see a man grappling with the problems of the bankruptcy of his nation. And come with an eloquent cry that we have nothing to fear but fear itself. But I wouldn't stop there. Strangely enough, I would turn to the Almighty, and say, "If you allow me to live just a few years in the second half of the twentieth century, I will be happy." Now that's a strange statement to make, because the world is all messed up. The nation is sick. Trouble is in the land. Confusion all around. That's a strange statement. But I know, somehow, that only when it is dark enough, can you see the stars. And I see God working in this period of the twentieth century in a way that men, in some strange way, are responding – something is happening in our world. The masses of people are rising up. And wherever they are assembled today, whether they are in Johannesburg, South Africa; Nairobi, Kenya; Accra, Ghana; New York City; Atlanta, Georgia; Jackson, Mississippi; or Memphis, Tennessee – the cry is always the same – "We want to be free."

◄ This is a famous quote of F.D. Roosevelt from his First Inaugural Address. What is the message for the audience in 1968?

◄ Mixing two continents. Is it the same fight?

And another reason that I'm happy to live in this period is that we have been forced to a point where we're going to have to grapple[3] with the problems that men have been trying to grapple with through history, but the demand didn't force them to do it. Survival demands that we grapple with them. Men, for years now, have been talking about war and peace. But now, no longer can they just talk about it. It is no longer a choice between violence and nonviolence in this world; it's nonviolence or nonexistence.

◄ Is this a civil rights issue?

That is where we are today. And also in the human rights revolution, if something isn't done, and in a hurry, to bring the colored peoples of the world out of their long years of poverty, their long years of hurt and neglect, the whole world is doomed. Now, I'm just happy that God has allowed me to live in this period, to see what is unfolding. And I'm happy that He's allowed me to be in Memphis.

▲ Is he talking about a material dream?

I can remember, I can remember when Negroes were just going around [...], so often, scratching where they didn't itch, and laughing when they were not tickled. But that day is all over. We mean business now, and we are determined to gain our rightful place in God's world.

And that's all this whole thing is about. We aren't engaged in any negative protest and in any negative arguments with anybody. We are saying that we are determined to be men. We are determined to be people. We are saying that we are God's children. And that we don't have to live like we are forced to live.

Now, what does all of this mean in this great period of history? It means that we've got to stay together. We've got to stay together and maintain unity. You know, whenever Pharaoh wanted to prolong the period of slavery in Egypt, he had a favorite, favorite formula for doing it. What was that? He kept the slaves fighting among themselves. But whenever the slaves get together, something happens in Pharaoh's court, and he cannot hold the slaves in slavery. When the slaves get together, that's the beginning of getting out of slavery. Now let us maintain unity. [...]

Now, let me say as I move to my conclusion that we've got to give ourselves to this struggle until the end. Nothing would be more tragic than to stop at this point, in Memphis. We've got to see it through. And when we have our

[3] **to grapple** to struggle to deal with sth.

march, you need to be there. Be concerned about your brother. You may not be on strike. But either we go up together, or we go down together. [...]
Let us rise up tonight with a greater readiness. Let us stand with a greater determination. And let us move on in these powerful days, these days of challenge to make America what it ought to be. We have an opportunity to make America a better nation. And I want to thank God, once more, for allowing me to be here with you. [...]
I left Atlanta this morning, and as we got started on the plane, there were six of us, the pilot said over the public address system, "We are sorry for the delay, but we have Dr. Martin Luther King on the plane. And to be sure that all of the bags were checked, and to be sure that nothing would be wrong with the plane, we had to check out everything carefully. And we've had the plane protected and guarded all night."

**Consider the message ▶ of the pilot. What is its intended effect?**

And then I got to Memphis. And some began to say the threats, or talk about the threats that were out. What would happen to me from some of our sick white brothers?
Well, I don't know what will happen now. We've got some difficult days ahead. But it doesn't matter with me now. Because I've been to the mountaintop. And I don't mind. Like anybody, I would like to live a long life. Longevity has its place. But I'm not concerned about that now. I just want to do God's will. And He's allowed me to go up to the mountain. And I've looked over. And I've seen the promised land. I may not get there with you. But I want you to know tonight, that we, as a people, will get to the promised land. And I'm happy, tonight. I'm not worried about anything. I'm not fearing any man. Mine eyes have seen the glory of the coming of the Lord.[4]

[4] quote taken from Julia Ward Howe, "Battle Hymn of the Republic", 1861

## Activities

Outlining the main ideas of the speech

1. Structure the speech and give appropriate headings.
2. In this speech Martin Luther King is looking back at what has been achieved and puts the fight into a global perspective. In groups draw a mind map of his main ideas. Compare your findings and agree on a common result.

Form and content

3. Outline the main stylistic devices used by Martin Luther King and explain their functions.

Handing down a message

4. It is the foreboding message of the last part of this speech (ll. 76–85) that made it famous. What sentiment does he express in this last part?
5. In pairs discuss his possible motivation for this message.

# Announcement of Martin Luther King's Death (April 4, 1968)

Robert F. Kennedy

Robert F. Kennedy (1925–1968) was a younger brother of John F. Kennedy. He worked as United States Attorney General[1] from 1961 to 1964, using his legal powers to sustain the Civil Rights Movement. He left the Johnson administration because he opposed the war in Vietnam and became Senator for the State of New York. In 1968 he ran as presidential candidate for the Democrats. He was assassinated on June 5, 1968 in Los Angeles.

Before you read/ listen

Imagine you are working for a newspaper and have just been informed about Martin Luther King's death. Use the information you have gathered before and write an obituary for him.

Martin Luther King (l.) and Robert Kennedy (r.)

Ladies and Gentlemen: I'm only going to talk to you just for a minute or so this evening, because I have some very sad news for all of you and, I think, sad news for all of our fellow citizens, and people who love peace all over the world; and that is that Martin Luther King was shot and was killed tonight in Memphis, Tennessee.

Martin Luther King dedicated his life to love and to justice between fellow human beings. He died in the cause of that effort. In this difficult day, in this difficult time for the United States, it's perhaps well to ask what kind of a nation we are and what direction we want to move in. For those of you who are black – considering the evidence evidently is that there were white people who were responsible – you can be filled with bitterness, and with hatred, and a desire for revenge.

We can move in that direction as a country, in greater polarization – black people amongst blacks, and white amongst whites, filled with hatred toward one another. Or we can make an effort, as Martin Luther King did, to understand, and to comprehend[2], and replace that violence, that stain of bloodshed that has spread across our land, with an effort to understand, compassion[3] and love.

For those of you who are black and are tempted to be filled with hatred and mistrust of the injustice of such an act, against all white people, I would only say that I can also feel in my own heart the same kind of feeling. I had a member of my family killed, but he was killed by a white man.

◀ **Allusion to whom?**

But we have to make an effort in the United States, we have to make an effort to understand, to get beyond, or go beyond these rather difficult times.

---

[1] **US Attorney General** *Justizminister* [2] **to comprehend** to fully understand
[3] **compassion** a strong feeling of sympathy for people who are suffering and a desire to help them

My favorite poem, my favorite poet was Aeschylus[4]. And he once wrote:

*"Even in our sleep, pain which cannot forget*
*falls drop by drop upon the heart,*
*until, in our own despair,*
*against our will,*
*comes wisdom*
*through the awful grace of God."*[5]

What we need in the United States is not division; what we need in the United States is not hatred; what we need in the United States is not violence and lawlessness, but is love and wisdom, and compassion toward one another, and a feeling of justice toward those who still suffer within our country, whether they be white or whether they be black.
So I ask you tonight to return home, to say a prayer for the family of Martin Luther King – yeah, it's true – but more importantly to say a prayer for our own country, which all of us love – a prayer for understanding and that compassion of which I spoke.
We can do well in this country. We will have difficult times. We've had difficult times in the past. And we will have difficult times in the future. It is not the end of violence; it is not the end of lawlessness; and it's not the end of disorder.
But the vast majority of white people and the vast majority of black people in this country, want to improve the quality of our life, and want justice for all human beings that abide[6] in our land.

**Remember that facing ▶ the great divide of the nation Lincoln used exactly the same expression.**

Let us dedicate ourselves to what the Greeks wrote so many years ago: to tame the savageness of man and make gentle the life of this world[7]. Let us dedicate ourselves to that, and say a prayer for our country and for our people.
Thank you very much.

---

[4] **Aeschylus** Greek poet and playwright (525 BC– 456 BC) [5] quote from Aeschylus, *Agamemnon*, 179–183 [6] **to abide** (*formal/old use*) to stay or live in a place [7] the quote is credited to Aeschylus by the Kennedy library, without giving any exact reference

## Activities

Summarizing the text

1. Imagine you were part of the audience. There was no written text of the speech. Tell a friend what Kennedy said.

Examine the composition of a spoken text

2. Compare your obituary with what Kennedy says. What are the common aspects and what is different? Make a list and discuss why Kennedy focuses on these aspects.

Considering the lasting effects of a speech

3. In this impromptu speech Robert Kennedy uses a number of stylistic devices that underline the message of his words. Make a list and explain the intended effect.

4. Checking Google or other search engines, you will find more than a thousand references to quotes from this speech, using parts of it in

blogs, articles or speeches. Which might be your favourite quote from this speech? Give reasons.

5. Robert F. Kennedy was shot and killed only two months later (June 5, 1968). In an obituary, *Time* magazine (June 14, 1968) used a quote from Aeschylus as its motto: "When the height is won, then there is ease." This evokes the image used by Martin Luther King ("I've been to the mountain top"). Is this one of the core beliefs of the American Dream? Discuss.

# "A More Perfect Union" (March 18, 2008)

Barack Obama

After Shirley Chisholm (1972) and Jesse Jackson (1984 and 1988) Barack Obama was the third Afro-American to run in a presidential campaign. He was the first to be nominated presidential candidate for the Democratic Party and was elected as the first Afro-American President of the United States on November 4th, 2008.

Before you read/ listen

Carefully describe the cartoon (from left to right). Summarize the message of the cartoon in a few sentences. Published at midterm of the presidential nomination campaign, does it support one of the two candidates (Barack Obama – Hillary Clinton)? Give reasons.

**The first words of the Constitution read: "We the People of the United States, in Order to form a more perfect Union."**

"We the people, in order to form a more perfect union."

**Why has he chosen ► Philadelphia for this speech?**

Two hundred and twenty one years ago, in a hall that still stands across the street, a group of men gathered and, with these simple words, launched America's improbable experiment in democracy. Farmers and scholars; statesmen and patriots who had traveled across an ocean to escape tyranny and persecution finally made real their declaration of independence at a Philadelphia convention that lasted through the spring of 1787.

**Barack Obama**

The document they produced was eventually signed but ultimately unfinished. It was stained by this nation's original sin[1] of slavery, a question that divided the colonies and brought the convention to a stalemate[2] until the founders chose to allow the slave trade to continue for at least twenty more years, and to leave any final resolution to future generations.

Of course, the answer to the slavery question was already embedded within our Constitution – a Constitution that had at its very core the ideal of equal citizenship under the law; a Constitution that promised its people liberty, and justice, and a union that could be and should be perfected over time.

**Which two persons are ► invoked?**

And yet words on a parchment[3] would not be enough to deliver slaves from bondage, or provide men and women of every color and creed[4] their full rights and obligations as citizens of the United States. What would be needed were Americans in successive generations who were willing to do their part – through protests and struggle, on the streets and in the courts, through a civil war and civil disobedience and always at great risk – to narrow that gap between the promise of our ideals and the reality of their time.

**Another immigrant's ▼ story?**

This was one of the tasks we set forth at the beginning of this campaign – to continue the long march of those who came before us, a march for a more just, more equal, more free, more caring and more prosperous America. I chose to run for the presidency at this moment in history because I believe deeply that we cannot solve the challenges of our time unless we solve them together – unless we perfect our union by understanding that we may have different stories, but we hold common hopes; that we may not look the same and we may not have come from the same place, but we all want to move in the same direction – towards a better future for our children and our grandchildren.

---

[1] **original sin** (religious belief) that man has a tendency to be evil from birth [2] **stalemate** a situation in which neither side can win or make any progress [3] **parchment** a thick yellowish kind of paper; (*here*) an old document [4] **creed** a set of principles or beliefs

This belief comes from my unyielding[5] faith in the decency and generosity of the American people. But it also comes from my own American story. I am the son of a black man from Kenya and a white woman from Kansas. I was raised with the help of a white grandfather who survived a Depression to serve in Patton's Army[6] during World War II and a white grandmother who worked on a bomber assembly line at Fort Leavenworth[7] while he was overseas. I've gone to some of the best schools in America and lived in one of the world's poorest nations. I am married to a black American who carries within her the blood of slaves and slaveowners – an inheritance we pass on to our two precious daughters. I have brothers, sisters, nieces, nephews, uncles and cousins, of every race and every hue[8], scattered across three continents, and for as long as I live, I will never forget that in no other country on Earth is my story even possible.

It's a story that hasn't made me the most conventional candidate. But it is a story that has seared[9] into my genetic makeup the idea that this nation is more than the sum of its parts that out of many, we are truly one[10]. [...]

**◂Think of how exceptional such a couple must have been at that time**

**◂Salad Bowl or Melting Pot?**

---

[5] **unyielding** sth. that does not fail or break [6] General George S. Patton, World War II general, commanding troops in Africa, Sicily and finally the Third Army from Normandy into Germany [7] **Fort Leavenworth,** Kansas founded in 1827, it is the oldest army post west of the Mississippi. [8] **hue** shade of colour [9] **to sear** to be burned into the surface of sth. [10] **out of many, [...] one** motto of the USA: *e(x) pluribus unum* (cf. p. 35)

## Activities

1. As an exchange student you watched the speech on TV. Write an e-mail in German to your friends at home, telling them what Barack Obama said.

   *What did he say?*

2. Obama's speech directly refers to American history. Make a list of the references and state why he has chosen them.

   *American history and the attitude of the presidential candidate*

3. Summarize in a drawing (genealogical tree) what Obama tells listeners about his family roots.

   *What is an American? Describing the roots*

4. Analyse the most important rhetorical devices used by the speaker to underline his message.

   *The rhetoric of a dreamer*

5. As Martin Luther King used a lot of allusions to the Bible in his speeches, Barack Obama directly or indirectly refers to other famous speeches, thus creating a net of argumentative ideas. Try to track down some of these references.

6. Obama claims that "in no other country on Earth is my story even possible." Is that true? Discuss in groups and write down your arguments.

   *Evaluating the message of the speech*

7. Prepare and stage a hot chair discussion with Barack Obama questioning his positions and views.

# Obama Makes History

Robert Barnes and Michael D. Shear

At the beginning of his campaign, Barack Obama's ideas were welcomed with less enthusiasm by the American press than by the overall positive European reactions. Have a look at the following cartoon published by *Newsweek* long before his nomination was decided.

Before you read

1. Describe the cartoon. Remember to stick to an objective description, just giving facts and no interpretation.
2. Describe in your own words what the cartoonist wanted to express.

Sen. Barack Obama of Illinois was elected the nation's 44th president yesterday, riding a reformist message of change and an inspirational exhortation[1] of hope to become the first African American to ascend to the White House.

Why the image of a ► "tide"?

Obama, 47, the son of a Kenyan father and a white mother from Kansas, led a tide of Democratic victories across the nation in defeating Republican Sen. John McCain of Arizona, a 26-year veteran of Washington who could not overcome his connections to President Bush's increasingly unpopular administration.

Standing before a crowd of more than 125,000 people who had waited for hours at Chicago's Grant Park, Obama acknowledged the accomplishment and the dreams of his supporters.

[1] **exhortation** *Ermunterung*

"If there is anyone out there who still doubts that America is a place where all things are possible, who still wonders if the dream of our founders is alive in our time, who still questions the power of our democracy, tonight is your answer," he said just before midnight Eastern time.

"The road ahead will be long. Our climb will be steep. We may not get there in one year or even one term, but America, I have never been more hopeful than I am tonight that we will get there. I promise you: We as a people will get there."

◄ **Note the "road" metaphor once again.**

The historic Election Day brought millions of new and sometimes tearful voters, long lines at polling places nationwide, and celebrations on street corners and in front of the White House. It ushered in[2] a new era of Democratic dominance in Congress, even though the party's quest for the 60 votes[3] needed for a veto-proof majority in the Senate remained in doubt early today. In the House, Democrats made major gains, adding to their already sizable advantage and returning them to a position of power that predates the 1994 Republican revolution.

Democrats will use their new legislative muscle to advance an economic and foreign policy agenda that Bush has largely blocked for eight years. Even when the party seized control of Congress two years ago, its razor-thin margin in the Senate had allowed Republicans to hinder its efforts.

◄ **Is this a completely positive image?**

McCain congratulated Obama in a phone call shortly after 11 p.m. and then delivered a gracious concession speech before his supporters in Phoenix. "We have had and argued our differences," he said of his rival, "and he has prevailed[4]."

"This is an historic election, and I recognize the special significance it has for African Americans and the special pride that must be theirs tonight," McCain said.

Obama became the first Democrat since Jimmy Carter in 1976 to receive more than 50 percent of the popular vote[5], and he made good on his pledge to transform the electoral map. [...]

Obama melded[6] the pride and aspirations of African Americans with a coalition of younger and disaffected voters drawn to his rhetorical style, and a unified base of Democrats worried about the economy and frustrated with the war in Iraq.

He is the fifth-youngest man elected to a first presidential term, after Theodore Roosevelt, John F. Kennedy, Bill Clinton and Ulysses S. Grant. He is the 16$^{th}$ senator to ascend to the office, and the first since Kennedy's election in 1960.

---

[2] **to usher in** *etw. einleiten; den Weg weisen* [3] the number is wrong, the correct number for a veto-proof majority is 67 [4] **to prevail** to defeat an opponent [5] **the popular vote** the real percentage of votes cast [6] **to meld** to combine, to blend two different things

## Activities

The reasons for success

1. Sum up the main reasons given in the article that helped Obama win the election.

A historical decision

2. The election is called "historic" several times in the text. Make a list of the facts about Barack Obama mentioned in the article that are special or even unique.

The Dream as a message

3. Listening or reading the many speeches Obama has given during the 2008 presidential campaign you will come across the "buzz"-words used in the cartoon. These were "hope", "believe", "change" and "dream". Looking back at the texts in this booklet, first draw a mind map of what "dream" stands for and then explain why this is the most powerful concept to win a majority of voters in the USA.

# Glossary

| Stylistic device | Example |
| --- | --- |
| **Alliteration:** repetition of a sound (usually a consonant) at the beginning of neighbouring words | "Somewhere at this very moment a child is **b**eing **b**orn in America. Let it be our cause to give that child a **h**appy **h**ome, a **h**ealthy family, and a **h**opeful future." Bill Clinton, *Democratic National Convention Acceptance Address,* 1992 |
| **Anaphora:** one or more words are repeated at the beginning of neighbouring sentences | "**We owe them** remembrance, and **we owe them** more. **We owe them**, and their children, and our own ...", George W. Bush, *Our country is strong,* 11.09.2002 |
| **Assonance:** identical vowel sounds in two or more words | "does that st**a**r-sp**a**ngled b**a**nner yet w**a**ve" |
| **Enumeration:** a list of three or more people, objects or ideas | "Our public interest **depends on private character, on civic duty** and **family bonds** and **basic fairness, on uncounted, unhonored acts of decency** which give direction to our freedom." George W. Bush, *1st Inaugural Address,* 2001 |
| **Euphemism:** the use of a mild or less negative word or expression to express something that is unpleasant or embarrassing | "he's been right here since he **passed away** (= died) last night", Stan Ridgway, *Camouflage,* 1986 |
| **Geminatio:** the doubling of words | "**No, no,** we are not satisfied, and we will not be satisfied", Martin Luther King, *I Have a Dream,* 1963 |
| **Hyperbole:** an overstatement or an intentional use of exaggeration | "The chamber is celebrating an important milestone this week: your 70th anniversary. **I remember the day you started**." Ronald Reagan, *Remarks at the Annual Meeting of the United States Chamber of Commerce*, 1982 |
| **Including 'we':** encloses the listener (I + you = we) | "**We** must forever conduct our struggle on the high plane of dignity and discipline." Martin Luther King, *I Have a Dream*, 1963 |
| **Inversion:** the syntactic reversal of the normal order of the words and phrases in a sentence | "And so, my fellow Americans, **ask not** what your country can do for you; ask what you can do for your country." John F. Kennedy, *Inaugural Address*, 1961 |
| **Litotes:** (opposite of hyperbole, s. a.) something that is presented as less important than it really is | "trust me, in my wife's family, that's **no small achievement**." Arnold Schwarzenegger, 2004 *Republican National Convention Address* |
| **Metaphor:** a comparison between two objects or ideas, without a word of comparison ("like", "as" or "as if") | "And if a **beachhead of cooperation** may push back the **jungle of suspicion**," John F. Kennedy, *Inaugural Address*, 1961 |

| | |
|---|---|
| **Metonymy:** a relationship in which one word or phrase is replaced by another closely related | "**The White House** announced the engagement yesterday," *Washington Post*, 16.08.2007 |
| **Onomatopoeia:** the use of a word which imitates the sound it refers to | "a bullet with my name on it came **buzzing** through a bush" Stan Ridgway, *Camouflage*, 1986 |
| **Parallelism:** a repetition of patterns of words or phrases | "Let every nation know, whether it wishes us well or ill, that we shall **pay any price, bear any burden, meet any hardship, support any friend, oppose any foe** to assure the survival and the success of liberty." John F. Kennedy, *Inaugural Address*, 1961 |
| **Personification:** gives an inanimate object human characteristics | "We are not this **story's author**, who fills time and eternity with his purpose." George W. Bush, *1st Inaugural Address*, 2001 |
| **Quotation:** an authentic word or phrase taken from a book, play, speech, etc. | "in the words of the old Negro spiritual, '**Free at last!** Free at last! Thank God Almighty, we are free at last!'" Martin Luther King, *I Have a Dream*, 1963 |
| **Repetition:** intentional repetition of the same or similar idea or language pattern | "**out of** step, **out of** arguments and just about **out of** time." Kofi Annan, *Washington Post*, 8.11.2006 |
| **Rhetorical question:** a kind of question that does not need to be answered, because the answer is obvious. | "Can anyone look at our reduced standing in the world today and say, 'Let's have four more years of this?'" Ronald Reagan, 1980 *Republican National Convention Acceptance Address* |
| **Simile:** a comparison between two objects or ideas, using "like", "as" or "as if" | "we will not be satisfied until justice rolls down **like** waters," Martin Luther King, *I Have a Dream*, 1963 |
| **Synonyms:** two words with (nearly) the same meaning | "George W. Bush has worked hard **to protect and preserve** the American dream," A. Schwarzenegger, 2004 *Republican National Convention Address* |

# Acknowledgements

## Texts

The Declaration of Independence (1776), Library of Congress, www.archives.gov/exhibits/charters/declaration.html, 24.11.08

The Bill of Rights (1791), Library of Congress, www.archives.gov/exhibits/charters/bill_of_rights.html, 24.11.08

Samuel Francis Smith: "America (The Beautiful)" (1832), Library of Congress, http://lcweb2.loc.gov/diglib/ihas/loc.natlib.ihas.100010476/default.html, 24.11.08

Francis Scott Key: "The Star-Spangled Banner" (1814), Library of Congress, www.loc.gov/exhibits/treasures/trm065.html, 24.11.08

Abraham Lincoln: "The Gettysburg Address" (1863), in: Henry Steele Commager: Documents of American History to 1898, Prentice Hall, New Jersey 1934

Bill Maher: "Taking What's Best from the French", from: Bill Maher, "Hillary Equals France," in *Newsweek International*, June 4, 2007

Frederick J. Turner: "The Significance of the Frontier in American History", in: The Annual Report of the American Historical Association for 1893, University of Wisconsin, pp. 199–227

Alexander Keyssar: "The West", in: Maier, Pauline et al.: *Inventing America*, Vol. 2, W. W. Norton, New York 2003, p. 582 f.

Mark Knopfler: "Telegraph Road", © Rondor Musikverlag GmbH, Berlin

John F. Kennedy: "The 'New' Frontier", Address at Rice University on the Nation's Space Effort, www.jfklibrary.org/Historical+Resources/Archives/Reference+Desk/Speeches/JFK/003P0F03SpaceEffort09121962.htm, 24.11.08

James Truslow Adams: "The American Dream", from: *The Epic of America*, Blue Ribbon Books, New York 1931, pp. 404, 405, 411, 412, 416

Janis Joplin, "Mercedes Benz", T+M by Janis Joplin/Michael McClure/Bob Neuwirth, © 1970 by Strong Arm Music, Sony/ATV Music Publishing (Germany GmbH), Berlin

Emma Lazarus, "The New Colossus", from: www.libertystatepark.com/emma.htm, 24.11.08

Joseph Bruchac: "Ellis Island", from: *Entering Onondaga*, Cold Mountain Press, Austin, Texas 1978

Amy Bloom: "And Lost There, a Golden Feather in a Foreign, Foreign Land", from: *Away*, Granta Books, London 2007, p. 7–9

Arnold Schwarzenegger: "Republican National Convention Address", www.americanrhetoric.com/speeches/convention2004/arnoldschwarzenegger2004rnc.htm, 24.11.08

T. C. Boyle: *The Tortilla Curtain*, Penguin, New York 1994

Gregory Rodriguez: "Migrate, then Integrate" in: *Los Angeles Times*, June 18, 2007

John McCain: Border Security and Immigration Reform, www.johnmccain.com/Informing/Issues/68db8157-d301-4e22-baf7-a70dd8416efa.htm, 24.11.08

John Steinbeck: *The Grapes of Wrath*, Penguin, Harmondsworth 1971, p. 35–37

Bruce Springsteen: "The Ghost of Tom Joad", © Springsteen Bruce Music, Rondor Musikverlag GmbH, Berlin

Daniel J. Kevles: "A Divided Society", in: Maier, Pauline et al.: *Inventing America*, Vol. 2, W. W. Norton, New York 2003, p. 999

Langston Hughes, "Harlem", from: *Montage of a Dream Deferred*, Henry Holt, New York 1951

Lorraine Hansberry: *A Raisin in the Sun*, Vintage Books, New York 1988, p. 133–135

Martin Luther King: "I Have Been to the Mountain Top", www.americanrhetoric.com/speeches/mlkivebeentothemountaintop.htm, 24.11.08, © Estate of Dr. Martin Luther King, Jr

Robert F. Kennedy: "Announcement of Martin Luther King's Death", www.historyplace.com/speeches/rfk.htm, 24.11.08

Barack Obama: "A More Perfect Union", http://my. barackobama.com/page/content/hisownwords, 24.11.08

Robert Barnes and Michael D. Shear: "Obama Makes History", in: *Washington Post*, 5.11.2008

## Illustrations

© dia/mediacolors: p. 4 top; © AP Photo/Khue Bui: p. 4 bottom r.; © ullstein bild – CARO/Muhs: p. 5 bottom; © AKG, Berlin: p. 7; © 2006 Florida Today: p. 10 top; © 2005 The Record New Jersey: p. 10 bottom; © H. Bauer: p. 11; © AP Photo/Gail Burton: p. 12; The Museum of Modern Art, New York: p. 13; Courtesy of The Bancroft Library. University of California, Berkeley: p. 14; © HBO: p. 15 bottom; © Christie's Images/CORBIS: p. 18; © orvalrochefort 2007/www.flickr.com: p. 22; © sandman 2007/www.flickr.com: p. 23 top; © picture-alliance/schroewig: p. 25; © AP Photo: p. 26; dpa: p. 27, 28; entnommen aus: Spiegel Spezial: Die wilden 68er. Nr. 1/1988, S. 13: p. 31; www.visitingdc.com: p. 36; © Random House, Inc.: p. 37; © picture-alliance/dpa: p. 39, 44, 48, 53, p. 66 bottom; Steve Breen, San Diego Tribune: p. 42; © H. Bauer: p. 43; © Russell Lee 1940: p. 51; © Fenno Jacobs 1942: p. 52; © OKAPIA: p. 55; © Schapowalow/Atlantide: p. 56; © US Postal Service 2002: p. 57; © Vintage Books 1994: p. 58; © 1961, Renewed 1989 Columbia Pictures Industries, Inc. All Rights Reserved.: p. 59; UPI/Bettmann Newsphotos: p. 60; © action press/ZUMA PRESS INC.: p. 63; Copyright © Time Inc. All Rights reserved.: p. 65 top; © Copyright 2008 John Darkow – All Rights Reserved.: p. 65 bottom; © Newsweek: p. 68; other illustrations: Verlagsarchiv Schöningh